Cary W. Jones

Norfolk as a business centre

Its principal industries and trades

Cary W. Jones

Norfolk as a business centre
Its principal industries and trades

ISBN/EAN: 9783744735780

Printed in Europe, USA, Canada, Australia, Japan

Cover: Foto ©Suzi / pixelio.de

More available books at **www.hansebooks.com**

NORFOLK

AS A

BUSINESS

CENTRE

Its Principal Industries and Trades.

CARY W. JONES.

C. HALL WINDSOR, BOOKSELLER AND STATIONER, No. 5 BANK STREET.

VIRGINIAN PRESSES, MAIN & COMMERCE STS.

1882.

NOTICE.

In bringing before the public the *third* annual issue of "Norfolk as a Business Centre," the publisher takes advantage of the opportunity thus presented, of stating that the publication for 1882 will be found to compare favourably with those of previous years. Both of the former issues attained a degree of popularity almost unprecedented with works of like character, and their circulation was very large and unquestionably benefitted the city. In view of these facts the publisher intends this year, as heretofore, to distribute gratuitously throughout this country and Europe, fifteen hundred copies. The first edition was met by an instantaneous and hearty recognition, which proved eventually to be but the precursor of the success which the second issue achieved, and which it is reasonable to expect will be even exceeded by that of the latest work.

Our business men recognizing its high value as an advertising medium, and appreciating the fact that its interesting reading matter and illustrations can not fail to secure for it a large circulation, have always accorded it an unhesitating and cordial support, and the extent of their patronage this year speaks best for itself.

NORFOLK.

1582—1882.

IN making our third annual bow to the business public, we feel that we come no longer as a diffident stranger seeking success and the applause of an unknown audience, but that the establishment of NORFOLK AS A BUSINESS CENTRE is an assured fact in whose glory we claim a share as in a measure, both its promoter and its result. In sketching Norfolk from its earliest times to the present we have little more to do, for the time prior to the year just past, than present a resume of the facts in our City's history so fully set forth in our earlier issues; and, then give more in detail what has been done in the past twelve months towards realizing our sanguine predictions of her rapid development towards that brilliant consummation, so devoutly to be wished for, of our hopes and wishes.

In 1582 Chesapik was a little Indian village situated on that beautiful arm of the sea, now known as Elizabeth River. There was little business doing here beyond the usual pursuits followed by the old men and squaws in the absence of the braves on their hunting, fishing or more war-like excursions. History represents the inhabitants of that region lying along the shores of the now called Elizabeth, down the line of the bay, past Lynnhaven, and out round the Capes, as very fierce and fond of incursions into the territories of neighboring tribes, and to accomplish this, it was necessary to provide transportation and this created a demand for boat building; and no more convenient spot could be found than the present site of that suburb of our city, Atlantic City, and right there commenced in a "pigmy way" an industry which will eventually be continued in the same locality on a gigantic scale. In 1584 a party of adventurous Englishmen, sent out under authority of good Queen Bess, by the gallant Raleigh, landed on Roanoke Island, now a part of North Carolina though then styled Virginia, and in one of their wanderings came across this Indian village of "Chesapik" and having reported its favorable situation to the Mother Country, Raleigh immediately divined the future of a town possessed of great natural advantages and gave his orders accordingly ; but history fails to give us the details of the unsuccessful attempt to plant here the first English settlement.

On the 8th of June, 1680, one hundred and eighty-eight years after the discovery of America, and seventy-three after the settlement of Jamestown, an Act of Assembly was passed which authorized the purchase of fifty acres of land for the town of Norfolk. In 1662, two hundred acres of the land now included in the city of Norfolk, belonged to Lewis Vandermull, who, that year, sold it to Nicholas Wise, Sr, a shipwright. The act for the purchase of this land was called "an Act for co-habitation and encouragement of trade and manufacture," and instructs that the price paid for " the land shalbe tenn thousand pounds of tobacco and caske, which sum the owner or owners thereof shalbe and are hereby constrained to accept, take, and receive, as free and valuable price for the said land forever." This act assigned to any person who would build a dwelling and warehouse upon it, half an acre of said land in fee simple, on payment to the country of one hundred pounds of tobacco and caske, the building to be commenced within three months after assignment. The act further required all produce of the colony to be brought to the warehouses established, one in each settlement under this act, for storage, sale or shipment, and the penalty for failure to comply with this act was a forfeiture of the products. The act also provided, that " all goods, wares, English servants, negroes, and other slaves and merchandise whatsoever that shalbe imported into this colony from and after the 29th of day September, which shalbe in the yeare 1681, shalbe landed on shore, bought and sould at such appointed places aforesaid, and at noe other place whatsoever, under like penalty and forfeiture thereof." Tobacco sent to these warehouses was exempt from all executions, attachments, &c. So important was the establishment of trade marts considered, that it was further provided that all who would "cohabitt, dwell and exercise their trades within the said appointed place," should be exempt from the arrest of their person or seizure of their property for debts previously contracted for five years, from the publication of this act.

On the 16th of August, 1682, the site of the present city was selected in "Lower Norfolk County, on Nicholas Wise, his land, on Eastern Branch of the Elizabeth River, at the entrance of the branch," and purchased from Nicholas Wise, a carpenter of Elizabeth River Parish and son of Nicholas Wise above named. Wise very *wisely* reserving for himself the site of his father's shipyard, which was identical with that of the triumphs of the aborigines in naval architecture. This fact is somewhat tastefully portryed on the original seal of the old "Borrough of Norfolk," in the representation of a ship on stocks in the foreground just beyond the city limits.

CUSTOM HOUSE.

The advantages of the situation had attracted so many to the new settlement, that in October, 1705; Norfolk was by Act of Assembly, established as a *Town*. The town of Norfolk continued to flourish until 1736, when by royal charter under date of September 15th of that year it was made a BOROUGH. The charter defined the duties of the Mayor, and other officials, and Samuel Boush was appointed Mayor, Sir John Randolph, Recorder, and John Newton, Samuel Boush, Jr., John Hutchings, Robert Tucker, John Taylor, Samuel Smith, Jr., James Ivey and Alexander Campbell, were named Aldermen. When the Borough was incorporated, its northern boundry ran from the cove at Town Bridge, (now the intersection of Church and Charlotte streets), in a westerly direction to the river, but in 1761 the limits were enlarged by an act of Assembly, so as to include " all the land south of a line running from the head of Newton's Creek, to the head of Smith's Creek." " In 1707 a new survey was ordered, and the line between the heads of the two creeks designated by stone landmarks." The jurisdiction of the city now extends over a space of about eight hundred acres.

On January 20th, 1832, the Virginia Assembly passed an act granting the freeholders of Norfolk the " privilege of electing the Mayor of the Borough."

On February 13th, 1845, by act of Assembly, the charter of Norfolk was altered and it became a CITY. From this time the commercial prosperity of Norfolk dates.

NORFOLK, the first city and chief seaport of Tidewater Virginia, is situated in lat. 36° 50′ 50″ N., long. 76° 18′ 47″ W., on the north side of an arm of the sea, called the Elizabeth River, and directly south of it on the opposite side of the river is the city of Portsmouth. But the port of Norfolk includes all the territory on both sides of the river, which embraces the cities of Norfolk and Portsmouth, the village of Berkley at the confluence of the Southern and Eastern branches of the Elizabeth and the suburban villages of Brambleton and Atlantic City, lying respectively above and below the corporate limits of Norfolk City. Within this territory now live 50,000 people.

Here we find a magnificent port with a channel approach of 28 feet water, thus open to vessels of the largest size and open too at all seasons, while it presents at all times a harbor safe, and free from prevailing epidemics. Eight miles below the city at Seawell's Point, the river flows into Hampton Roads, which is unsurpassed, if not unequalled as a harbor in the World.

The following is its official description as furnished by the U. S. Coast Survey:

" Hampton Roadstead is formed by the confluence of the James, Nansemond and Elizabeth rivers, and is bounded on the north by Old Point Comfort and the Hampton shore to Newport's News; on the east by a line drawn from Old Point Comfort Lighthouse to the Rip Raps, and continued to the west end of Willoughby bank ; on the south by Willoughby Bay and Seawell's Point Spit; and on the southwest and west by a line drawn from Seawell's Point to Newport News Point. Between these limits the Roads are about four miles long, with a depth from four to fifteen fathoms and excellent holding ground. At the eastern boundary the anchorage is three-quarters of a mile wide, and gradually widens towards the southwestward until abreast of the western end of Hampton Bar, where it is a mile and three-eights wide, between the lines of three fathoms." To realize to the full the capacity of this grand harbor for the world's shipping, we must not forget that the nautical mile referred to above 2,028 yards, or over 15 per cent. more than the statute mile.

Beginning its existence as City, as we have said, in 1845, immediate prosperity seems to have attended its new state, as shown by the increase in the assessed value of Real Estate, the rapid growth of its trade and

Hygeia Hotel, Old Point Comfort, Va.
Harrison Phoebus, Proprietor.

the development of a spirit of enterprise, which soon launched the new city into a current of progress. At that time, its only avenue of communication with the interior, besides its country roads, were the natural ones furnished by the waters tributary to the Chesapeake, and the Dismal Swamp Canal, connecting it with the Sounds of North Carolina and the rivers emptying into them. This Canal was opened in the year 1828, the United States Government and the State of Virginia being its largest stockholders, and for many years it has poured into the lap of Norfolk a large and renumerative trade in lumber and naval stores. Of recent years this Canal has been burdened by a large debt, and recently it was sold to satisfy the lien of the bondholders, and purchased at a very reasonable price by a company of wealthy citizens of Norfolk and others, who are making all the improvements necessary to its successful and profitable working. Running as it does through one of the finest lumber regions in the world, and connecting with the Sounds of North Carolina, the business that will pass over it must be large and profitable to those who purchased it.

In 1858, the Norfolk and Petersburg Railroad was begun, and in 1859 it was completed to Petersburg, where it met the Southside Road to Lynchburg, and there connected with the Virginia and Tennessee Road to Bristol. A diversity of interests, prior to the late war, arising from a distinct and separate management kept them however from doing anything but a way business.

It was in the present century that our city had reached a relative position as a port that has not yet been reached in her present palmy days of commercial success. The oldest inhabitant of to-day and many creditable witnesses who have but recently passed away, recalled with pride the time some seventy years ago when it was not only a possibility but an accomplished fact to walk from Norfolk to Portsmouth on the decks of vessels loading at our wharves. But Jefferson's embargo and other unfavorable legislation turned the tide of trade from our shores, and our commerce sickened and languished almost to death.

Staves, lumber, shingles and corn, from the swamps and fruit lands of the neighboring counties of North Carolina, found a market in Norfolk and helped to raise many of our citizens to wealth in domestic trade as the West Indies business did in the foreign. The Irish famine of 1847, drew upon our resources as a corn market and gave a lively spurt to our foreign commerce, which has only been rivalled by our more recent efforts in that direction ; and very large seemed those vessels to our eyes then as unloaded they loomed above our wharves, though doubtless they would appear but pigmies besides the monarchs of the sea that now bear full loads of cotton from our shores.

In 1854 and the early part of 1855, our city gave every promise of taking a front rank in the march of progress. In the former year, that great improvement, which now has a most prominent place in our water front, the Boston Wharf, was begun by two of our most enterprising citizens, since gathered to their fathers. But in 1855 the prosperity of Norfolk received a serious check from the Yellow Fever Epidemic of that year, which, stopped for a time all business and carried off a large portion of our population, among them several of our most enterprising citizens, whose efforts for her prosperity have been as sadly missed since their loss, as they had been shown in her progress during their life.

Hardly had our city recovered from the almost crushing effects of the Yellow Fever, when the war in 1861 again prostrated her commerce and closed her port.

The Summer of '65, while it found active hostilities at an end, and our people once more gathered in their old homes, seeking employment in such avocations as seemed most likely to yield a provision for themselves and families, came upon our city in a state of comparative isolation from all her old connections. Her railroads were cut off from their termini, while her lines of water transportation were principally new or in the hands of indifferent outsiders and used merely to earn the most money possible in carrying visitors to the late fields and scenes of war, or else in furnishing supplies for the surrounding country, still suffering from the exhaustion of war.

FIGHT OF THE MERRIMAC AND THE MONITOR.
From Butler's Pictorial History U. S.

Monitor to the Left.   Merrimac to the Right.

The good people of the neighboring counties, lying on the North Carolina sounds, who had formerly sought in our city a market for their rich yield of corn, found the vast supplies of grain, which the new developments of our "Iron Age" were bringing from the overflowing granaries of the fruitful West, precluded thought of rivalry and therefore ceased to cultivate that product of their soil and began to feel the first symptoms of the cotton fever, which has revolutionized the agriculture of that section of the old North State.

In the year 1866 was seen the dawning of a brighter day for the commercial prospects of our city in the advent of direct trade between our port and Europe, while our trade with the West Indies, which had once been not only large but a fruitful source of profit to our Norfolk merchants, was partiallly resumed. A review of our foreign trade for the fifteen years ending with the Winter 1880-81, the details of which we have not space to repeat in this volume, revealed the fact that its growth had been marked and considered as a whole, most favorable and yet by no means without fluctuations and in fact, in some of its branches this trade had shown a decided decline.   The effort of importation had proved a failure, having subsided into a few cargoes of salt and an occasional one of fruit.

The shipment of staves to the West Indies, a business conducted by three of our leading firms, which in 1875 had attained very respectable proportions, the exports that year being valued at $405,446 have year by year declined until those of the last year referred to show an aggregate value of $167,900, which is less than any year since 1866.   This decline, however, we think, is owing to the decrease in the demand in the West Indies, and in consequence of a falling off in the yield and export of rum, sugar and molasses from these islands and Demerara, and also from the use of second-hand staves, as there is no other source from which they could derive such staves as our market has always afforded and for which it is justly celebrated.

In 1875 our exports of grain (Indian Corn) were valued at $111,800 ; and showed a handsome increase in the two following years, reaching a climax in the latter of $246,426.   In 1881 they amounted to only $144,247, which was a trifling advance, however, on their value for the preceding year.   This is not a matter of wonder, however, when we consider the wonderful facilities for handling and loading grain at Baltimore, and remember that there is a centripetal force in trade which can be only overcome by some other and greater pressure brought to bear upon it.

We miss, too, the advent of the immigrant direct to our shores, an advantage we enjoyed when the Allen Line, then calling at our port on their route from Liverpool to Baltimore, from May, 1872, to May, 1874, landed here 2,292 persons from the Old World, seeking homes in the New.   With unusual facilities as a point for the distribution of immigrants—for our means of transportation to the interior are unrivalled as to cheapness and unsurpassed as to comfort and dispatch—it seems but just that we should have our full share of the benefits of this incoming tide of immigration.   These settlers are no pauper herd coming down upon us as the locusts of Egypt to devour the substance of our goodly land, or seeking to deprive our own people of employment.   They all bring something and oftimes infuse new life and energy into a community, and are willing to take up just those burdens of life that our own people are unwilling to bear, or are just ready to lay down from exhaustion.

Even though our State has failed to make practical use of those means suggested to her by which immigration to her borders might be induced and fostered, and consequently few may tarry just yet in Old Virginia, their passage through our city will be an advantage. For some trifle is sure to be dropped by the wayside, and the little left behind by each will soon come to aggregate the much.

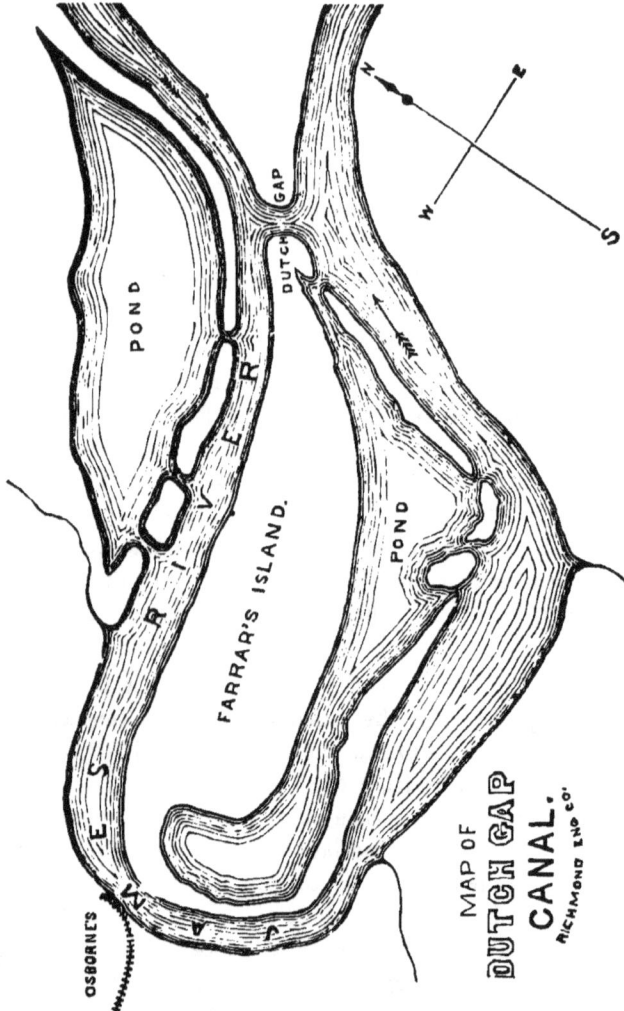

POND

RIVER

FARRAR'S ISLAND.

DUTCH GAP

POND

OSBORNE'S

MAP OF
DUTCH GAP
CANAL.
RICHMOND ENG CO.

But while the decline in certain branches of trade seems discouraging, there is no denying that since the year 1873 our growth as a cotton port has not only been steady, but perfectly wonderful, and we stand to-day, according to the statistics not only the third port in receipts of cotton

(713,026 bales), but *second only to New Orleans in direct shipment to Great Britain* (316,046 bales), at the conclusion of the year 1881.

In 1871 the tonnage required to carry our direct exports amounted to 10,398, which has steadily increased, if we except the year 1877, until it reaches a very handsome figure for 1881. These figures, we think, exhibit most strikingly the tremendous increase in our foreign trade.

The trans-atlantic shipment of timber and lumber has grown to be quite an item of our trade since 1877. Beginning in that year with a valuation of $47,709, the figures the year 1880 reached $84,375, with the trade just in a vigorous infancy, and destined to an enormous increase, by the active aid of those great feeders of trade that are busily at work bringing the products of the interior to the ships lying at our wharves, ready to carry them to foreign markets. From the same sources we have also obtained a trade in manganese ore, which, in its fifth year, has reached a valuation of $50,649. But despite this handsome exhibit of the tonnage required for our exports and the strong probability of a continued increase in the demand, there is a lack of symmetry in our foreign commerce. It needs some of the elements which would make it an established and permanent direct trade. Liverpool is the one grand centre to which, with but few exceptions, our whole commercial intercourse is tending. This we fear is an element of weakness and we long to see the day when the grand trans-atlantic line, with Norfolk and Flushing as the terminal points—the line pointed out by Maury—shall be an accomplished fact, and no pent up island, but the whole continent shall not only receive but reciprocate our shipments. We must also have a further development of the grain and timber trade, putting us in direct communication with other continental ports, and thus remedy this otherwise serious defect in our foreign commerce.

We find this noteworthy and gratifying fact brought to light by examing our Norfolk cotton statistics for the first half year of the season 1881–82, ending February 28th, that while the gross receipts show a falling off as compared with those for the same period of the previous year, it seems to be only the common experience of cotton ports and has not lost us our relative rank ; but the most pleasing feature is that the entire loss in the receipts of cotton is for through shipments coastwise, while there is a small increase, some 900 bales, in the receipts of cotton to be handled directly at this port.

The foreign shipments, while short to this date nearly 5,000 bales, showed a larger comparative deficiency in the early part of the year and bid fair before its completion to exceed those of the past season, a most legitimate result of our greatly improved facilities for handling and forwarding this staple, which will be more fully alluded to, when we come to give in detail the many improvements that the past twelve months have developed in our city.

In a former edition, while paying a just tribute to our admirable Cotton Exchange; which, in the past year has added fresh laurels to a well-earned reputation, and done noble work in furthering the claims of our Virginia seaport as the gate to the highway of the seas for the cotton sisterhood of States, by the admirable and effective presentation of facts and figures to the assembled representatives to King Cotton's congress at Atlanta, last Winter, through her eloquent and able President sustained by an enterprising and public-spirited delegation of his confreres; we urged the necessity of a more general combination of our business men

RUINS OF THE OLD CHURCH AT JAMESTOWN.

One mouldering tower, overgrown with ivy, shows
Where first Virginia's Capital arose,
And to the tourist's vision far withdrawn
Stands like a sentry at the gates of dawn.
The church has perished—faint the lines and dim
Of those whose voices raised the choral hymn;
Go read the record on the mossy stone,
'Tis brief and sad—oblivion claims its own.

Thompson's Virginia.

from all the branches of trade and commerce, whose object and aim should be to practically present such a taking view of the advantages of Norfolk as a Grand Business Centre as would draw representative men, both buyers and sellers, from the British Isles and the Continent of Europe, as well as from our Southern section, whose natural market we are, to come and establish a cosmopolitan entrepot here at Norfolk, more especially for the Southern Atlantic Coast. The port of New York, however large and enterprising, however vast may be its resources, is wholly incapable of doing the business on its Atlantic Coast of this vast empire that now contains over 50,000,000 people, and extends from ocean to ocean, and trade will inevitably seek another outlet, so soon as the rising tide reaches its flood, bursts over the barriers that vainly attempt to check its progress and will flow in that channel and towards that point at which the most earnest efforts have been made to prepare a way for it. Now we congratulate our city that the primary steps were taken last February, and in the right direction, when a Business Exchange was inaugurated ; but rightly believing that to win the coveted success strength and thorough organization were needed, a committee of thoroughly practical business men was appointed to confer with a like committee from the Cotton Exchange, for the organization of a Business Exchange as complete and thorough in all its departments as our present Exchange is in its specialty, from which we have every reason to hope in the near future, brilliant results in the more rapid advance of our city in all branches of business towards its ultimate rank as one of the beacon lights of commerce on our Atlantic front.

We, of Virginia, like many people and all individuals who have a past, are fond of overhauling the musty records to find out what wonderful future is buried in the bosom of some deep, quiet lake, hidden in the recesses of some dark forest where the light of God's sun has scarcely penetrated or shall be brought forth by the noisy labor in its babblings of some mountain stream, seeking to loose itself in the impulse of instinct in some far-off vast ocean of whose very existence it is practically ignorant, or shall spring forth from those bogs and marshes, at once mother and home to those phantom will-o-the-wisps that have led us all astray oftimes in our boyhood, according to the prophetic vision of some time-honored sage. To those who still listen to the syren-like songs of these old legends, it may be a pleasure to know that nearly one hundred years ago, one Thomas Jefferson, whose principles, now perhaps, are more honored in the breach than the observance, prophesied that " Norfolk will probably be the emporium for all the trade of the Chesapeake Bay and its waters, and a canal of eight or ten miles will bring to it all that of the Albemarle Sound and its waters." And chiming in with our sage as if to aid to bring about his prophecy, we find another from our neighboring state, to which Norfolk is so closely added by the ties of consanguinity as well as trade, advising her people in view of the unfitness of her south-eastern coast for commerce, to avoid it and throw their whole energy into agriculture and manufacture.

It remained for one of our latter-day sages, eminently practical, though not so full perhaps of brilliant theories and glittering generalties, and who lives, we are happy to say to enjoy the fruits of his enterprise and skill; and long may he live and long may the broad pennant of our genial Commodore wave o'er the barks that float on the brave waters he has done so much to keep in motion! to make the two cuts out of the old mothers—Virginia and Carolina—that should open the way to a closer and fuller commercial alliance between their children.   In a word, the

U. S. NAVAL HOSPITAL.

Albemarle and Chesapeake Canal not only is and has been of inestimable value to our city as a great feeder of trade, but is likely to continue to increase in usefulness, destined as it is to become a link in that great chain of water communication, which binds the whole eastern front of our common country.

With the same waters of our natural allies, the North Carolinians we are connected by an older water-way, now a nonagenarian; for it was early in the nineties of the last century that this useful enterprise was begun; running right through the great Dismal Swamp, with its tangled juniper, from whence it took its name—"Dismal Swamp Canal." It was one of our Norfolk pets for a long time and has had no little hand in a quiet way in adding to the wealth of many of our citizens and the general prosperity of our city. Uncle Sam was largely interested in it, too, at one time, having expended nearly $1,000,000 upon its enlargement and improvement. The matter of its construction and continuance being considered of such importance as to elicit both national and state aid. During the civil war this work was a great sufferer for having been used extensively by both Governments, Confederate and United States, it was finally abandoned by the latter, when it had completed its mission for them, and left to its fate. The result, on the return of peace, was that in the then depleted condition of their finances, nothing could be done by the stockholders but to borrow money on the work, which was accordingly done and the Canal once more opened to navigation. Further pecuniary aid being required to raise it to a standard commensurate with the demands of a growing trade, appeals were made to the United States for assistance, which had become absolutely necessary to the prosperity of the work. Failing to receive it, a foreclosure of the mortgage bonds ensued resulting in the sale of the canal and its reorganization on a firm basis free from the trammels of Governmental control. The experience of the past year has fully shown the benefits of this change, and with an outlay of $50,000 and under the management of a thoroughly practical and experienced superintendent, who gives his whole time and attention to the important work, the business and resources of the Dismal Swamp Canal has been quadrupled in the past year and it now bids fair to regain its ancient prestige and to realize all the brightest anticipations of its friends and patrons. One of our wealthiest and most liberal-minded citizens, seconded by a public-spirited directory, is President of the Company and ably and fully sustains the Superintendent in his efforts to make the Canal a public benefit. In this connection a first-class steam service has been introduced on the canal under the auspices of this company and is meeting with merited success. The depth of water in the Canal is now kept up above the standard minimum of its charter and will eventually be brought to that of the national standard for ship canals.

Before passing from the water-ways, that aid to bring up the trade and commerce of our City, to the great iron roads that are fast driving it out of its selfish isolation—as the best fed city of America—it is but justice to our position as a " City of Waters " as well as to the numerous excellent steam lines that ply to and from Norfolk to give at least a brief mention of each of them and their various connections. The line which perhaps is now taking the most conspicuous place from its connection with the

various Railroad companies that find a Seaboard terminus in our city
and therefore claims first mention is the OLD DOMINION STEAMSHIP
COMPANY, which connects us with the great metropolis of our country—
New York—and which for something over a decade has admirably met
the demands of trade with its fine fleet of coastwise steamers, three times
a week or oftener when occasion required, besides numerous auxiliaries
that ply the waters of the various streams, which flow into the Chesapeake, and thus help to swell the great bulk of the products of the soil
that find their market in our midst. This line already owns some fifteen
steam vessels and in the month of March two fine steamers were launched
at one of the great Philadelphia Shipyards, which will further increase

DISCIPLIS' CHURCH—FREEMASON STREET BET. BANK AND BREWER.

its ability to meet the demands of the public. In February last in consequence of the expiration of the contract with the Messrs. Clyde & Co.,
to leave the Old Dominion Steamship Company undisturbed on their
route from New York to Norfolk and Richmond, the Norfolk and
Western, the Seaboard and Roanoke and Chesapeake and Ohio Railroads
formed a combination and purchased a controlling interest in this line,
as a measure of self protection and in the interest of Norfolk's trade.
For the present the same service will be continued and virtually under
the same management—over which however through its directory these
roads will in a measure exercise a control. It is proposed so soon as the
Chesapeake and Ohio Railroad complete their extensive works at their
deep water terminus—Newport News—to have a daily line from Norfolk

via the News to New York, dispensing with the Richmond route, which
has proved at times both inconvenient and expensive.

The old "Bay Line" continues to give us a daily passenger steamer
with an increased modicum of freight boats and keeps up its reputation
of being in more senses than one, a great feeder.

The Clydes give us direct steam communication with Philadelphia,
besides the usual net work of minor lines permeating the adjacent country
and aiding to sustain the main one by the products brought therefrom.
Connecting us with the Cities of New England and her Cotton Mills,
the Merchants' and Miners' Transportation Company is ever affording
increased facilities for business in its season and pleasure for those who
seek recreation during the heated term.

All these steam lines are links of that great chain between the Atlantic
and the Mississippi which is formed by junction at Norfolk with the N.
and W. R. R.

We have also an excellent daily line of steamers to the National
Capital and a tri-weekly one to that of our own State, while the name is
legion of the smaller craft steam and sail, which pour into our market
the rich yield of our neighbors.

But Norfolk's first love—her first venture in Railroads, at least so far
as having the Iron horse snorting and cavourting along her very streets
and not a little to the dismay and disgust of many of her old fogey inhabitants, was the Norfolk and Petersburg R. R.   All of her older citizens
remember the advent among us of that little man with a mighty spirit
who was to control its destinies and to make it one of the best if not the
very best built road in the country.   Many a contractor had to "squeal"
under his decisions—but the Road when completed was a source of pride,
pleasure and eventually profit to its Stockholders and every man, woman
and child along its line.   It was the conception of the same great mind
to enlarge this germ into the grand idea of consolidation which under his
regime was completed to Bristol, on the Tennessee line, under the title of
the A. M. & O. R. R.   Adverse circumstances, in the shape of the terrible financial panic and consequent crisis of 1873 and hostile bondholders,
who could neither foresee the result nor appreciate the utility of a home
protecting policy but sought first and last to realize their pound of flesh
forced the road into the hands of Receivers.   A kind but mysterious
Providence so ordered events that the business manager selected to conduct affairs under the new Regime was the able and trusted lieutenant of
the great captain of consolidation.   With a return of more prosperous
times, the Road seemed on the eve of being returned to its original pro-

jectors, but in the judgment of those controlling the matter a sale was deemed expedient and the result has proved most beneficial to all concerned. The new company under the name of the Norfolk and Western Railroad has now perfected its title, the contract having been confirmed by the Virginia Legislature at its last session and approved by the Governor, February 19, 1882. The balance of the purchase money was paid into the treasury and the State has released in full all claim which she holds against the organization. This removes the last cloud on the title. It is a source of pride to our people to feel that the great lines which reach the deep waters on our shores are beginning to bear the name of our city

EXCHANGE NATIONAL BANK—MAIN STREET.

by the sea, and it is significant fact witnessing that we are no longer a secondary consideration in the policy of these lines. And the grand idea is now being urged of beginning at Norfolk and stretching out briarean arms not alone to the Ohio, nor the Mississippi but westward with the Star of Empire to the Pacific Slope.

While its shops and principal business offices are at Lynchburg, the central point of the N. & W. R. R. proper, but which will probably be removed to Roanoke its junction with the Shenandoah Valley R. R., in reality a part of the same great combination, inside of a year, the grand objective point of this Road must be Norfolk, as that towards which all movements for an extended trade with the transatlantic world will have to be made, and as events, we think, will prove the more convenient way for making its Eastern connections; as the means of handling freight at Norfolk and the water transportation therefrom grow to be commensurate with the progress of the times. As an evidence of the regard in which our city is held by the new organization, we can point to the wonderful improvement that has taken place at the station grounds and depot of this Road at Norfolk; for the visitor returning after an absence of twelve months will fail to recognize in the handsome and commodious accommodations that now welcome the traveller any resemblance to the old dilapidated shanties that have nearly entirely disappeared and will have completely done so by the next Summer. And this is but a minor portion of the improvement; the disappearance of that old relic the Norfolk drawbridge has taken place and now an unbroken wharf-front of nearly one-third of a mile with ample depth of water all the property of this Road presents itself. Large storehouses have already been erected, others are projected while a still greater supply only waits on the demand. One of the most important uses to which this improvement will be put is in affording a depot at Norfolk for transmitting the abundant products of coal and other minerals of which the region adjoining the N. & W. R. R. to the west of Lynchburg is most prolific. The New River branch road to the coal mines is now completed and this is but one of the three roads projected by the company to the mining districts.

President Tyler of the N. & W. R. R., thinks when his connections are completed with this almost inexhaustible mineral region, Norfolk will stand unsurpassed as a coal market on the Atlantic coast. But the N. & W. R. R. proper is only one link in that powerful chain which was formed last Fall by the inauguration on the 1st October 1881, of the tripartite contract for joint traffic management made between the N. & W. R., E. T. V. & Ga. System or combination and the Shenandoah Valley R. R., and which promises most advantageous results. Under this contract for twenty-five years remarks President Tyler, "the line of the N. & W. is practically extended and direct connection secured with Chattanooga, Memphis, Savannah, Montgomery, Mobile, New Orleans, Harrisburg, Philadelphia, Baltimore and New York," and we may add through the water connections at Norfolk, all ready alluded to, with the cities and mills of New England. We are thus closely allied with the great Cole or Georgia system which is rapidly pushing its efforts to make up for the great disappointment in losing the Cincinnati Southern and which will we hope before long succeed in building up to the Kentucky Central and thus recover the lost ground.

The same able and live management that raised up the unfortunate A., M. & O. R. R. after better times financially dawned upon the country, not only controls the N. & W. R. R. but also this new organization. And what is its destiny? Surely not to terminate in a great Atlantic and Mississippi line; but spanning the Father of waters at Memphis, when an earnest and irresistable appeal to a liberal minded Congress shall have brought Government aid to this great national highway to the Pacific, unimpeded by the snows of Winter, it will find its western terminus at San Diego, California, or some other favorably located point on the Pacific Coast. This is no idle dreaming, for results far less practicable in their seeming not a score of years ago are now being consummated.

ACADEMY, AND NORFOLK LIBRARY ASSOCIATION BUILDING.
Bank, Charlotte and Cumberland Streets.

In connection with the Air Line we would briefly allude to its claim and trace office, which has its headquarters in Norfolk and is conducted by that genial gentleman Walter T. Payne, supported by an intelligent corps of clerks. This office has not only charge of claims and traces, as its name would indicate, but has the management at Norfolk of the important and growing business of the foreign shipment of cotton. By the skill and good judgment of the gentleman in charge during the season ending with August last 75,000 bales of cotton and upwards were shipped from the Interior via Norfolk or about three eights of the entire cotton which reached Norfolk over the N. & W. R. R. We learn with regret that it has been seriously advocated, more in the interest we think of another locality than of the Line at large, to remove this important office from Norfolk, and we trust our new Business Exchange will inaugurate a career of promised usefulness by taking such immediate steps as will prevent such an unfortunate move. We feel sure that if some of our leading men, whose judgment would have weight with the manager of the Line, would briefly present the manifold benefits to result from retaining this office and its present agent at Norfolk, the necessity of having him convenient as a claim agent to this important point of most general and difficult transfers on the Line and more especially to the further development of that large and growing foreign business, so successfully conducted by him, even the discussion of such an impolitic step would be stopped at once and forever.

Another excellent move under the auspices of this Road is the establishment of an Immigration and Mining Bureau, an important matter, in which through her Railroads our Sister State, North Carolina, has gotten decidedly ahead of us. This Bureau has been established by J. B. Austin, at Wytheville, Va., and sanctioned by the N. & W. and S. V. R. R's. By or before the first of June, it is expected the Shenandoah Valley R. R. will be completed to Roanoke and the joint improvements there will have so far progressed as to permit the removal of the principal office of this Bureau to that point. A Monthly Bulletin of properties for sale will be issued for circulation among investors, manufacturers and agriculturists, and with the new facilities for reaching these points by the N. & W. R. R. and its branches, there is little or no doubt that a liberal policy on the part of our people, will cause a flood of immigration of that better sort that adds impetus to the progress of a community and brings wealth, or at least material benefits to all concerned.

Before leaving the subject of the N. & W. R. R., we must not neglect a reference to the " Norfolk Terminal Co.," organized March 16, 1882, under an act of the Legislature, approved March 6, which will, we have no doubt, contribute largely to the growth and material prosperity of our city. Its incorporators and present directors are the following well known gentlemen :—Messrs. Boyce, Kimball, Tyler, Clark, Doran, Jones, Billups, Lamb and Portlock; the majority of whom are identified with the N. & W. and Shenandoah Valley Railroads, and two of the number equally so with most of the schemes of the last ten or fifteen years for our city's advancement, and we are sure no better guarantee could be given that the Company means business, real and active, than its being under the control of such a management, with F. J. Kimball, Esq., at its head.

This Company has the right to construct, own and operate a railway with all necessary tracks, siding and branches, from any point on the N. & W. Railroad, in the county of Norfolk, to any point or points at or near the harbor of Norfolk on Chesapeake Bay, in the counties of Norfolk and Princess Anne. It is also authorized to construct at or near the harbor of Norfolk, wharves, docks, warehouses, elevators and cotton presses, suitable for the accommodation of steamships and vessels, and for the convenience of shipping, transporting and storing all kinds of merchandise and property, and the Company may conduct a general dock, wharf, warehouse, steamship and lighterage business.

SEABOARD COTTON PRESS (REYNOLDS BROS,) TOWN POINT.

This Company is also authorized to consolidate with the N. & W. Railroad and connect and unite physically with the railway of any other existing company upon such terms as may be agreed upon. It has also the further power to issue mortgage bonds, secured by its property and franchises, whenever the directors may deem it expedient to do so for the prosecution and extension of its work.

Its minimum capital of $100,000 may be increased to $5,000,000, and under its charter all rights and privileges thereof are forfeited by a failure to expend within two years, in the designated improvements, the amount of this minimum capital. Through this organization we look forward at no distant day to seeing the accomplishment of our plan proposed last season, of a great depot, docks and warehouses, established at

the site of old Fort Norfolk for our foreign business in all its aspects.
Further, we think, the far-seeing and enterprising gentlemen, who constitute the management of the Terminal Company, will at an early day
get possession of the former "Vue de l'Eau" property, connect it by
rail with the N. & W. R.R., and there establish docks for coaling purposes,
followed by an elevator and a cotton press and large warehouses.   Once
having the outports established there on a firm basis, we will be prepared
to see our city, by rapid growth both up and down the river, in an almost incredibly short time, form a continuous line, though of course for
many years an attenuated one, from Campostella bridge to Seawell's Point.

But we fear that our interest in this subject has made us dwell too
long upon this very important motor towards our present high rank
as a Business Centre, and we must now turn to a consideration of her more
ancient ally whose terminus is on the Southern side of our harbor—the
SEABOARD & ROANOKE R. R.   Under its old name and with almost
unvarying success this road has fought its way through times and tides
of fortunes that its less happily constituted neighbors have had to suc-
cumb to.   It is the connecting link between Norfolk and the whole
system of Roads throughout the South Atlantic and Gulf States, and is
one of the main arteries of our trade.   With its connections in the former, it makes the "Atlantic Coast Line," while with those in the latter,
it forms what is known as the "Seaboard Air Line."   It has not only
a magnificent business from the interior in cotton, of which it has been
the largest transporter to our market, but does an excellent carrying
business to that section in return.   And no better evidence of this can
be furnished than the completion of those really vast improvements and
facilities for increased trade which were referred to as projected in our
former edition.   Not satisfied with the erection of immense warehouses
which have already stored several millions bags of fertilizers from this
market and the northern ones, to be carried into the country from which
the cotton and other crops will be brought in due time in exchange, to
say nothing of other articles of produce and merchandise ; and adding
to their terminus on the Southern side of the harbor extensive dock
facilities aggregating a frontage of 500 yards ; they have purchased on
the Norfolk side, at a first cost of nearly $30,000, a valuable site for a
wharf and dock on an extensive scale which they shortly propose
to improve in keeping with the advanced business ideas of the day.

Nor is it alone at this terminus of the line that the system of which
this Road is but a small section is making progress.   This management
controls the intermediate road between the Piedmont Air Line and the

coast line of Railroads, taking it to Raleigh via Hamlet on the S. C.
line. It has recently acquired the Carolina Central Road from Wilmington to Charlotte through Hamlet; will push a connection to Cheraw
and Chester, S. C., and thence to Newberry, and will then be prepared

HOSPITAL St. VINCENT DE PAUL—CHURCH AND WOOD STREETS.

to strike a decisive blow to regain much of its lost ground and even
advance into the territory of its formidable enemy the Piedmont Air
Line, dividing its splendid cotton trade and bringing that staple right to
our doors. This connection when all its lines are complete, will make
almost an air line between Atlanta and Norfolk, through a region most

prolific of cotton. Mr. Robinson, the controlling genius of this system, has, we are told, the most unlimited confidence in the Port of Norfolk as having the superior advantages for shipping cotton. It is interesting to note in this connection that the master spirits of these great lines that are seeking to make or rather take advantage of the coming greatness of Norfolk as a Port, are actuated by no favorable prejudices towards it, but are drawn to seek it by an uncontrollable impulse which savours strongly of destiny or overrulling Providence.

Scarcely a year ago, the booming of cannon announced the completion of that brand-new applicant for public favor, the Elizabeth City and Norfolk R. R., which modestly located its depot in the village of Berkley, on the southern branch of the Elizabeth River. The site, we think, was admirably chosen as being most convenient in all respects and affording opportunity to extend their wharf facilities as it became necessary. Already they have completed their extensive docks and wharves at first contemplated, but with their steadily growing and healthy business these will soon be entirely inadaquate to meet the pressing demands of commerce. The Northern division of this Road extended to Elizabeth City, a distance of 43 miles, but the Road has now been completed to Edenton, some 30 miles further, thus realizing one of the great expectations of Norfolk merchants before the war ; a circumstance which would then have been hailed with a jubilee, but which now is almost overlooked in the ardor of our race for greatness. We note with pleasure that with the extension of this Road there seems to come a most pressing necessity for further advance. The modest title of the Road has been dropped and we now welcome the Norfolk and Southern Railroad as another great supporter of our City in her march of progress. One of our North Carolina Journals, compliments very highly and justly, we think, the management of this Road, on the splendid success which has rewarded its skill and enterprise, while making the statement, that notwithstanding they had equipped the Road in a manner which they deemed amply sufficient, they find that they are compelled to increase the rolling stock in order that they may be enabled to supply the demand made on them by the continuous run of freights, daily increasing in magnitude. Nor is it local trade alone that keeps up this Road, but their connections here are very complete for through shipments and it possesses the great advantage in having three busy seasons, trucking, fishing and cotton. We learn that it is contemplated to connect Edenton by steam ferriage with Plymouth and Jamesville, still further up the Sound, and from thence by a short road already built, to reach Washington and to push rapidly the construction of their line from that point to Newberne, while its ultimate Southern terminus will probably be some point in Florida, on the Gulf of Mexico. We have often heard it claimed by the good people of the Old North State that Norfolk fairly belonged to them and in view of this rapidly growing connection and the recent acquisition in the interest of Norfolk of the Carolina Central, we feel that we shall be so tightly grappled to their hearts by bands of steel that per force they will come and take us anyhow. Or we would propose as a com-

BIRD'S EYE VIEW OF HARBOR.

promise that they unite with us to build such a great city here that it will be too large to be claimed entirely by any one State, but be the great metropolis of the South.

We come now to speak of the last of the great overland routes in whose success the interests of our City are more or less involved—the Chesapeake and Ohio R. R. The great benefits to Norfolk from this Road are still a future contingency, and may even prove a remote one. But that there is a future for us in the completion of this Road and

its extensive improvements at its deep water terminus, Newport News,
no one will deny who has closely studied the question.

The earnings of this Road during the past year over and above current expenses were considerable, though more than absorbed by the
extraordinary outlay occasioned by re-laying the whole line of road with
steel rails.   In our last edition this Road was reported as operating 432
miles, to which it has since added its Peninsula extension of about 75 miles.
In addition to this it has increased its Western connections considerably,

VIEW OF HARBOR, WITH NAVY YARD IN THE DISTANCE.

and reaches by these alliances Louisville, Cincinnati, Chicago, Memphis
and other leading cities in the West, Northwest and Southwest.   Its
eastern terminus is still, practically, however Richmond, Va., and will
continue so until the completion of its large docks, storehouses, &c., at
Newport News.   Here will be an extensive coaling station and an elevator with a capacity for 1,500,000 bushels of grain, and terminal facilities
generally for the products of the West, and when completed it will be
necessarily connected with our city by ferry barges, so that capitalists,

prefering Norfolk, with its many and growing advantages, as a residence, will be able to use the "News" for business purposes as the merchants of Baltimore use Locust Point.

There remains only to be considered of the Railroads in which Norfolk is materially interested, the two which for the present, at least, will contribute as much to her pleasure as profit; we refer to the Ocean View Railroad, extending from this city about 8 miles to the hotel of the Ocean View Hotel Co., by whom this Railroad is owned. It has been very successful for two years past as a means of Summer travel, and as afford-

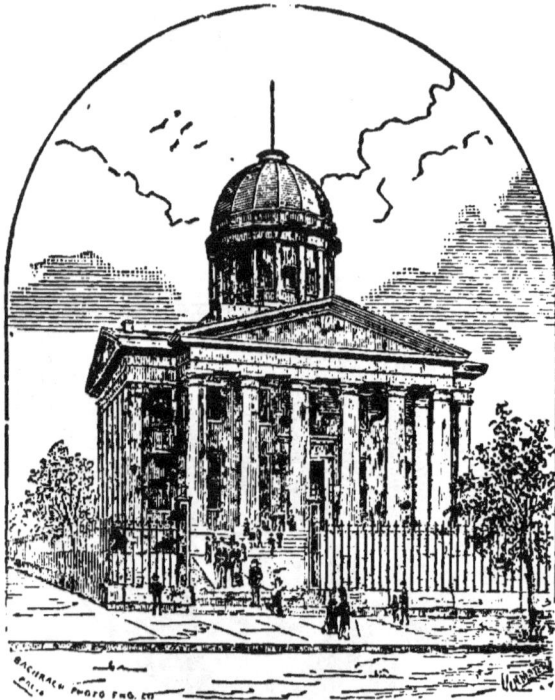

CITY HALL AND COURT HOUSE.

ing a short and inexpensive trip during the heated term to those who have only time in the evening to steal away from business for a few hours, and bids fair in the coming season to be equally well patronized.

The other Road is the "Norfolk and Virginia Beach Railroad," which, just at present, is merely prospective. For many years the "Hollies," immediately on the Atlantic Ocean, has been known as a most favorable location for a Summer Hotel, but the experience of the Hygeia Hotel, at Fortress Monroe, has taught us the lesson that visitors from the far West, flying the rigors of their unbearable Winters, find in this latitude,

on the sea-coast, where the seasons are modified by the close proximity
of the Gulf Stream the great climatic desideratum. It is said the Proprietor of the Hygeia had to refuse during the past Winter over 300
such applicants, while keeping his house, with accommodations for nearly
1000 guests, full nearly all the time.

Two years ago, an enterprising dealer in real estate in our midst, succeeded in bringing the facts regarding this locality to the attention of
Northern capitalists, who came, saw and were conquered ; and the result
is the purchase of 6 miles of the finest ocean beach on the Atlantic coast,
with lands adjacent, at a cost of about $25,000. Upon this will be
erected in the course of the next eighteen months a magnificent Sea Side
Hotel, designed by one of the first Architects of the country, and capable of accommodating comfortably 800 or more guests. The lands in

HOME SAVINGS BANK—MAIN STREET AND ROANOKE AVE.

the vicinity are to be laid off in convenient sized lots which will be disposed off on reasonable terms to purchasers, who agree to improve them
at once.

This Company organized under the amended charter of the Norfolk
and Seawell's Point Railroad, will proceed as soon as the Spring opens to
construct the Norfolk and Virginia Beach Railroad, for which they have
the route surveyed and mapped and the right of way secured, and everything ready financially and otherwise to complete the Road in sixty days
from first breaking ground. It will be run from Brambleton, in the
vicinity of the N. & W. R. R., in a bee line, shortly after leaving that
point, 17 miles to the " Hollies." It is hoped the work will be sufficiently completed by June 1st, to commence the shipment of material
for the Hotel, as of course nothing can be done on the building until

transportion is provided. The Company hopes by the 4th of July next, to have made sufficient advance to allow pic-nic parties a trip to the Ocean with some sort of temporary accommodations for the day, and by the next anniversary to have their magnificent hotel fully opened to the visiting world. With just an easy ride of an hour from the Ocean to Norfolk, the restless tourist after breaking his fast to the music of old Ocean's roar, may take the N. & W. R. R., and after a day's jaunt sup "on some blue mountain of the Old Dominion," and vice versa.

MAIN STREET—ATLANTIC TO COMMERCE STREETS, NORTH SIDE.

Turning from the consideration of our land approaches to that of the advantages for water communication with the outside world, it is a matter of no little surprise that a liberal and progressive Government should have treated with absolute neglect one of its finest harbors naturally, while lavishing its money in vain attempts to make or improve harbors which have scarcely a claim to the name of port. Although regaining possession of Norfolk and its Navy Yard early in the late war (May

1862) and making most valuable use of it as a rendevous and more or
less injuring its harbor by using it as a naval anchorage, not one penny
was ever subscribed towards its improvements by the United States Government for eleven years after peace was made, though it was well known
that it had been deteriorated and was still deteriorating.   In February
1875, an act of the Legislature established a Harbor Commisson and after
strenous efforts of local and State authorites a pitiful appropriation of some
$35,000 was procured and similar sums have been doled out for the past

MAIN STREET—ATLANTIC TO BANK STREETS.

six years aggregating less than one quarter million of dollars.   Careful surveys of the harbor and wonderful improvement in the approaches and
harbor proper have been made by a judicious outlay, considering the
small amount available, but much remains to be done to restore our harbor to its pristine glory and to place it in such a condition as to prevent its
retrograding.   We would respectfully urge our city authorities to make a
more strenous effort and more earnestly back up our representatives in

Congress in their efforts to obtain an appropriation commensurate with our importance as one of the leading seaports and naval stations of our great country. And we think the efforts to help ourselves as evinced by the wonderful growth and improvement of our water front fully merits a more favorable consideration on the part of the Representatives of the nation.

NORFOLK STEAM BAKERY, 87 MAIN STREET—JAMES REID & CO.

We read of the rapid growth and improvement of the cities of the West, that almost spring up in a night like the mushroom, but in the conservative east, especially in our staid old commonwealth, and more especially in that " pokey old fish and oyster town, " whilom the synonym for slow, the honorable President of the Cotton Exchange must have taxed the credulity of his hearers when he gravely announced to the Cotton and Railroad magnates at Atlanta, that the demands of trade had been so great as to compel the construction in our harbor within the past year of nearly three miles of new wharf front, an addition unequalled in the whole of the 75 years preceeding. But it is a positive fact and the figures aggregated after being gathered from reliable sources showed this extension to be 14,580 feet. And more than this immense warehouses have been built upon them and the demand is still for more. We find our predictions in this respect and in others either realized or in process of realization. To-day we have six powerful compresses in operation, whose daily capacity reaches 10,000 bales. Three of them belong to the Seaboard Compress

J. M. BUTT'S, Nos. 4 AND 6 AND WEBB, JETT & COX'S, No. 8 MARKET SQUARE.

Company, two of which were working twelve months ago and the third a new one erected on the Southern side of our harbor. The Virginia Compress Company, which had the misfortune to lose its compress by the fire in March 1881, owns the fourth, the "Mastadon of Compresses" said to be the largest and most powerful in existence readily squeezing two large bales into a little one. Then the Shipper's Compress Company, which is a new organization this season, has one on the Portsmouth side and one on the great McCullough improvement in Norfolk.

Giving employment to these compresses we have seventeen shippers to foreign ports, all members of our Cotton Exchange and some of them representatives of the wealthiest cotton houses of the world.

Apropos of these improvements while not wishing to discriminate among our citizens, all of whom we believe are gradually imbibing the new spirit of enterprise and progress which is fast gaining a permanent control of our community, we think it but justice to refer specially to the great work which has been done by A. A. McCullough in transforming the unsightly flats west of Stone Bridge and Granby street into one of the busiest localities of our city.

The original scheme proposed and advocated in our city councils and referred to by us last year was postponed and would in all probability

PURCELL HOUSE, MAIN AND CHURCH STREETS—R. T. JAMES.

have been postponed indefinitely till quietly forgotten but private energy and enterprise took hold of the matter and as if, by magic, that old receptacle of the filth of sewerage, busy only with that life of corruption which the sun light awakened in the tide-left mud flats, is changed into a busy depot of trade and commerce. In a single year this improvement has added sixty acres of land to the area of our city with wharves and warehouses, while a sufficiently deep and broad canal running east and west up to Granby street, makes a secure dock for vessels of a large size

to a point west of Stone Bridge where it is crossed by a drawbridge over
which pass the cotton loaded cars consigned to the Shipper's Compress
via the N. & W. R. R.

While the increase of the commerce and trade of our city has been so
encouraging we regret not to be able to record a proportionate increase in
manufactures which we think so necessary to preserve a healthy equili-
brium. Not that we are totally deficient in that respect for our Cotton

ST. PAUL'S CHURCH—ERECTED IN 1739.

Factory having been rebuilt is in full operation, but then it is one, when
it should be one among many, and in a town or city, we should perhaps call
it, like ours where we have a considerable preponderance of females, it is
most essential to the preservation of health and morals that we have
healthy and respectable, and at the same time remunerative employment of this character in abundance.

It used to be the want of fresh, pure water that was the great obstacle
to the establishment of manufactories in our midst, but that defect was
remedied some nine years ago by the introduction of water by the Holly

system and an appropriation has been recently made for increasing the supply, and steps are being accordingly taken in that direction to an almost indefinite extent. But before leaving the subject of manufactures we must not fail to allude to the successful ventures in making fertilizers by several of our leading firms, who are constantly extending their business, increasing their own wealth and adding most materially to the prosperity of our city. Moreover by the seeker after information scattered through the now somewhat confined limits of our corporation, will be found many successful and growing manufactories that escape the eye of the casual observer, but which bear strong evidence of a fast developing move towards

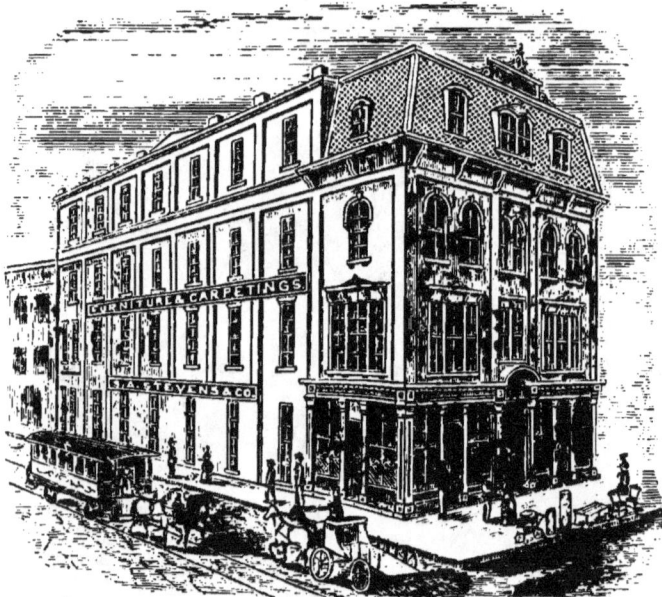

S. A. STEVENS & CO.'S.—MAIN AND GRANBY STREETS.

the establishment of such improvements. There are many opportunities of investments in this line awaiting the advent of capitalists to take advantage of them. While on this subject it may not be amiss to recur to the Peanut Factories of which we have three large and flourishing ones in our midst using the most improved machinery and employing hundreds of hands principally females and boys and turning out by their cleaning process a nut which stands unrivalled in the market. As is perhaps now generally known Virginia is the largest peanut growing State in the Union and Norfolk is par excellence the peanut market of Virginia, in fact of the world. Our trade in that article amounting to nearly one and

a half million of dollars and our shipments North, South and West reaching some 1,200,000 bushels. No considerable effort has been yet made
towards a foreign shipment of this article but we have no doubt that

JAMES POWER & CO.'S—26 and 28 ROWLAND'S WHARF.

a judicious testing of the market would result in time in quite an active
trade.

Somehow while speaking of peanuts and *vice versa* our mind invariably
reverts to oysters, whether because they are naturally classed together as
shell-fruits or because they are among our earliest youthful tastes and

pleasures we can not tell, enough that the subject is brought up and in passing merits at least a brief mention. The gathering, shucking and preparing for shipment of this most popular edible is not only an element of business strength and substantial profit to the capitalists who invest largely in this business, but is most useful in its employment of several thousand of that vast laboring horde in whose employment the nation finds peace and whose idleness brings anarchy and revolution. Not less than one and a half millions of bushels of these bivalves find their way from our market to all parts of the world, until the "Norfolk Oysters" have grown to be "household words" alike in the log cabin of the Western hunter and the palace of the Eastern Prince. Still another industry in-

M. A. & C. A. SANTOS'—MAIN AND ATLANTIC STREETS.

vites our attention; which fills our harbor with sail and steam vessels of various sizes engaged in the transportation of lumber, first towed down to the various mills, which dot the numerous branches and creeks that empty into our river, in the crude state of logs, often in huge rafts that for a time seem to impede navigation and there sawed and shipped away or consumed at home to meet the daily increasing demand for houseroom and making in all a business which exceeds two millions of dollars.

There is evidence everywhere of new life in our city's business and the day of stagnation we trust is numbered among the irrevocable things of the past, indeed we are sure of it, if our wide awake and liberal minded merchants and capitalists will give a long pull, and a strong pull and a pull altogether and keep the ball in motion.

We will now return to the water question, which at one time grew to be a serious detriment to our city's advance, as every continued drought then entailed not only inconvenience but sometimes little short of positive suffering. All this has now been remedied and the rapid increase which is being made in the use of what is known as the City Water is gratifying.

Not only as a necessity for the ordinary purposes of every day life and the establishment and perpetuity of manufactories but as essential to our protection against conflagration has this introduction of water proved an inestimable benefit. By its free and practical use our Fire Department are made most efficient as proven by their successful efforts in quelling the devouring element in March, 1881, when the Cotton Press of the Virginia Compress Company was destroyed and a large section of the business portion of our city was in imminent danger. Every means seems to have been taken which the facilities available can afford for the protection of property, especially in those portions of the town where cotton and other combustible matter is stored. Not feeling ourselves altogether competent to suggest any decided improvements in the system now in vogue, we would still modestly urge our city Fathers to establish telegraphic alarms through our city, as many as might be deemed best in each of the six fire districts, after due consultation, and located at the most important points. The key to each alarm being deposited with a responsible party livnig at the most convenient point adjacent. Let each alarm have its number. Then when the warder at the City Hall receives the signal from the Fire Department which is first notified, he will strike the bell from one to six, according to the district, then after a breathing space he will strike the bell from one to — according to the station in that district nearest the fire. In this way each citizen hearing the alarm will be notified of the exact location and know how far his interest may require his presence there.

It does not come within our province to discuss the healthiness or unhealthiness of our Atlantic Coast and its towns and cities; it is enough to say that our city has a record that will compare favorably with any of them in the matter of health, and the only serious epidemic that has ever prevailed in our midst occurred some twenty-seven years ago, and was introduced by a vessel from foreign parts which was permitted to slip through a quarantine, which has since been more rigidly enforced, in a season of overwhelming confidence induced by a preceeding Summer so healthy that its small mortality was phenomenal. This much we will permit ourselves to say that when we consider that a supply of water for general use has now been introduced into our city about nine years, with a steady increase each year in its consumption, with no adequate means at hand or provided to remove the superfluous fluid necessarily resulting

NORFOLK, VA.

R. S. DODSON,

PROPRIETOR.

New Atlantic Hotel

therefrom, but on the contrary, in the march of improvement, much new ground has been made, in some instances, filling up the natural drains, it is a matter of wonderment and conclusively proves the salubrity of our climate that no serious and permanent ill effects have resulted.

In our former edition, we alluded to the appointment of a committee by our City Councils to consult with an eminent Sanitary Engineer, in order to adopt a proper plan for effecting such drainage as might be best suited for our soil and topography, and a preliminary report was submitted to them in April, 1881, and a further report was furnished in June by Maj. Geo. E. Waring, and was referred to the New Councils who came into office on the first of the next July. That no serious results were apprehended by our city fathers from delay in acting upon the matter must be inferred from the fact that over six months elapsed —the fall and best half of the Winter being allowed to pass—before this important work was commenced. The system of drainage adopted is very similar to that in use in Memphis, and has to recommend it both the practical success in that city, where it has been thoroughly tested and found efficient and the name of its projector, which stands justly pre-eminent in his specialty. "Fortunately," he remarks, in referring to this subject, " the subsoil of Norfolk is very largely of a porous character, and the simplest means of underdrainage will be much more effective there than they would be in a more uniformly retentive subsoil." This work has now been commenced in earnest and will be pushed as rapidly as possible until the season becomes too far advanced for such a general upturning of the soil to be permitted, and then will be resumed with the first frosts of the Fall, and continued to completion. We believe, with one of our practical scholars, that Norfolk will only require, in connection with this system of drainage in order to give it its proper sanitary rank among the cities of our Country, that the landlords generally supply their tenants, especially the poorest, with our city water, and fill up all those holes in the ground where a large mass of our colored people, and many white ones too, have to get the water they use in the outskirts of the city, and that the city fathers grade the street gutters and make them impervious to water. There is no doubt a full supply of pure water readily attainable and as easily gotten rid of when made use of will greatly conduce to the health and comfort of the recipients.

To those who seek a change of scene and climate during the heated term when every one needs more or less relaxation, we know of no place which has more to recommend it as a residence than our city. Less than twelve hours ride on the comfortable coaches of the N. & W. R.R., brings the tourist to the charming mountain localities of our own state, while the Ocean View and Virginia Beach Roads, within an hour put him either on the shores of the inviting Chesapeake or of the broad old Ocean, as he may prefer. There is also communication several times a

day with Fort Monroe, where he will find that very popular and well-kept house, the Hygeia Hotel, open Summer and Winter, most attractive in itself besides the additional attractions in its immediate vicinity, of the most extensive and strongest fort in the United States, always well garrisoned, and in the near neighborhood the old town of Hampton, so full of interest to the visitor; the Soldier's Home and that admirable educational institution the Normal School, which is doing so much for the intellectual and moral training of the colored race as well as the Indian. The Old Dominion Steamers give a twenty-four hours taste of the outside trip to those wishing a little sea experience or this time may be increased to forty-eight hours or longer, and the traveller taken within a short ride of the White Mountains, if desired, by the M. & M. Trans. Co.'s Steamers to Boston. In fact we are placed in ready communication with almost every part of our common country by one or the other of our admirable Rail or Water Routes.

But there are those whose limited means forbid even a short Summer jaunt and these are often the very ones who most need change from the crowded thoroughfares of the city to some quiet and pleasant spot within easy reach on foot. It is for these we would make a most earnest appeal to that branch of our City Government whose duty it is we think, as well as privilege, to make such provision. We have witnessed with pleasure in the last few years of our city's existence, that a persistent effort has been made by some at least of our younger citizens to throw off the yoke of old fogyism and in so doing while giving all due reverence to the hoary head they have shown a quiet determination to have a will of their own and to find a way for that will. It is to their enterprise and push we must look for the consummation at an early day of the scheme to open spaces and reservations, filled with shade trees and green sward, with neat fountains cooling and refreshing the surrounding atmosphere with their spray, at various points within the present limits of our city; but here the matter must not rest but outside the present boundaries and no better place, we think, than just over Drummond's bridge, a tract of land, a few acres at first to be gradually increased, should be procured and the iniatory steps taken towards giving our people that great sanitary desideratum, a Park.

In this connection the present Chief Magistrate of our city speaks, we think, both wisely and well in his last annual message to the Councils accompanying the reports of the various city officers :

"Now that we have an abundant supply of good water, nothing our Councils could do, after securing the Waring system of sewerage and drainage, would contribute to the wealth, health comfort and moral purity of our community, than the establishment of a Park at some eligible point within a reasonable distance of our corporate limits.   Every dollar invested in such an improvement, would add tenfold to the value of our city property.   A beautiful Park adds to the attractiveness of a city, makes it more desirable as a place of residence, and is a strong induce- ment to people of wealth and culture to make it their home.   Besides the pecuniary advantages of a Park to a community, there should be a higher incentive, in providing the people with a place of recreation, where they can enjoy freedom from labor, where pleasant rides and walks, green lawns and the attractions of nature and art, invite mirth and gladness, and provide healthful amusements."

A nother outcrop of this same spirit, which is the harbinger of that coming future, the star of whose glory still glimmers but mistily on the verge of our horizon, is the taking up of our suggestion as to a consolida- ted corporation.   Of course a natural pride is causing a temporary rebel- lion against this scheme on the part of those who are to be ultimately the most thoroughly benefitted thereby, and a short-sighted policy sees no further than the slight inconvenience of increased taxation, and over- looks the immense benefits rapidly accruing in the near future.   Unques- tionably the consolidation and if necessary the extension of our joint limits to Tanner's Creek and in time to Seawell's Point, as must inevita- bly be the ultimate result if in the future our commerce demands a propor- tionate increase of water-front, would give us a place among the fifty important cities, in respect to population, our absence from which in our present stage of advance is a terrible disadvantage.   Naturally one hear- ing of Norfolk examines this list and unfavorably notes that we are not there.   A consultation perhaps of a Railroad Guide gives us a position as the terminus of several Railroads and we are classed with other similar points North, South, East and West, as a speculative venture and not being out in the progressive West by no means an inviting one. Again an epicure will remember and perhaps suggest Norfolk fish and oysters, which while delightful in their way may give us even a lower status on the commercial scale.

How then shall we drop our provincialism and take proper rank among the cities of this vast and growing continent?   Consolidate, we say, and let a community of interests break down all the petty jealousies and rivalries that now so unhappily prevent or at least retard any joint suc- cessful efforts.   In a little while we will find that though expenses have been increased, we do not feel them, for the benefits accruing to the whole by consolidation will have given a larger population and an increased value to our properties, personal and real, that will more than meet the demand without increased taxation; and our town people will gladly give way to the demands of business now almost pushing them to the walls in the present narrow confines of our city, and seek freer and healthier homes in the added territory from which the idea of moving into the country now

YORKTOWN CENTENNIAL.

Principal arch, erected at Market Square, to commemorate the Surrrender of
Lord Cornwallis at Yorktown, Oct. 19th, 1781.
Celebrated in Norfolk October 21st, 1881, by a general holiday, civic and
military parades.

excludes them; while our rural friends, will keep the freedom of their country homes with the added pleasures and profits of city residences.

And just here let us speak of Norfolk's finances. It is a source of gratification and pride to our citizens that amid the general business prosperity and growth of our city, that the credit of the corporation has been well sustained and the Finance Committee of the Councils, which retired on the 30th of June, 1881, have the proud consciousness of having so well performed their duty as to fund over a half million of our city's indebtedness at a much lower rate of interest, and of establishing a sinking fund that in less than thirty-seven years will enable us to pay off our entire present indebtedness, and this too without making any allowance for the increase in population and value of property which seems inevitable in the light of our present improved business prospects. Our 5 per cent. city bonds are to-day worth a premium.

But what shall we call our new city? Certainly by the older name, the City of Norfolk. With the exception perhaps of our sister city of Portsmouth, the neighboring localities would hardly object to this nomenclature ; and will her good people let a sentiment stand in the way of substantial prosperity? They should remember our port is now best known as the harbor of Norfolk, and even the Navy Yard is now the Norfolk Yard ; moreover they are not the " portsmouth " but Seawell's Point is their rival for that appellation. We think the torch has been applied to the old fossil relics and though the damp and mildew may make them smoulder for a while, the time is near at hand when their blazing pyre will mark the course of progress and consolidation hand in hand and our united people with one heart and voice will exclaim in the language of one of our Southern literati:—"Sink the microcosm in the infinite macrocosm. Perish the segregate in the boundless, rushing, choral aggregation."

There are two events in the history of the past twelve months which we think bring out in clear and well defined characters the fact that our people are well up with the advanced genius and progressive spirit of the times, and in closing this sketch we must be pardoned if we seem to dwell upon them too long. The one awoke the spirit of sadness and cast a gloom over every heart and home of our common country, while the other awoke a joyful memory of a glad time, a hundred years ago, without which perhaps our Country had never found place or name among the nations of the earth.

Last year, as every American must know, who is not unmindful of the history and glory of his country, was the centenniary of the Yorktown surrender, and through the energy and enterprise of M. Glennan, Esq., of the *Norfolk Virginian,* a movement was inaugurated, the result of which was a celebration of this important event in the nation's career. A preliminary meeting at Yorktown, on the 19th of October, 1879, had given the movement the necessary impetus, which was seconded by various local organizations in several of the States, most interested in the event. The meeting in Norfolk looking towards an active participation in the celebration by preparing a welcome to our city of the numerous guests to the Centennial in transit through our midst, was held at the call of Mayor Lamb, March 31st, 1881, and followed up eventually to a complete success by the energetic and liberal minded committees then appointed. But upon

ST. MARY'S CHURCH—HOLT AND CHAPEL STREETS.

this preparation for a joyful celebration fell like a funeral pall that saddest and most disgraceful act in American history, the assassination of her President in the heart of her Capital in time of perfect peace. The lingering illness and subsequent death of the Nation's Chief of course threw a damper upon all preparations for festivities.

We doubt if in any city of the land the news of our President's death was more quickly spread and more deeply felt than in our city by the sea, for the solemn pealing of the bells just an hour before midnight on

that 19th day of September, sounded a knell which warned every heart
that heard of the sad tidings. The man of business going to his work
next morning or the stranger strolling for pleasure, was met at every
turn by the outward manifestations of a universal sorrow, nearly every
building, private and public, being draped in mourning.

On the next evening the people assembled en masse to tender their
condolence to the afflicted, mingled with their just indignation against
the foul deed of the assassin. We are sure that the true spirit or great
heart of our people never more clearly revealed itself. Space forbids
us to dwell on this sad picture even had we the inclination, and we turn
to a brighter aspect of the national spirit of our community.

Feeling that unpropititious circumstances and its unfavorable location
combined to make the celebration at Yorktown far from the success
which the occasion merited, it became our people to make an effort
to impress more favorably the visitor with Virginia spirit and enterprise
than could be done by the crude display at Yorktown, and remove in fact
a feeling of prejudice and disgust that would naturally arise from disap-
pointed expectations ; and to this end a sufficiently ample appropriation
was sought and obtained from the corporate authorities, to which was
added liberal donations by our citizens at large. On the 11th of October a proclamation by the Mayor was issued requesting an active participation by all citizens in a week of festivities, commencing with Monday,
October 15th. He particularly invited the large fleet of British
vessels lying at our wharves to participate in this celebration as they now
gave our port "a great victory of peace, instead of the dread alarm of
war which the British fleet created one hundred years ago." And it
was wonderful to see how our people burying " the great sorrow " in the
depths of their hearts, went into the " mad gayety " of the hour with
almost the abandon of the Latin race.

On our principal thoroughfare were three handsome triumphal arches
adorned with appropriate pictures and inscriptions. The first at the
Atlantic Hotel corner, the central one, just opposite the market space and
the third at the Purcell House corner. Every store was covered with bunt-
ing, while crossed lines from the various principal buildings were almost
loaded down with flags, and many private residences vied with the public buildings in the beauty of their adornments. At intervals during the
day fine bands discoursed inspiring strains from stands erected for that
purpose at several convenient localities, extending their performance late
into the night, amid the glare of electric lights which were scattered
profusely over the city. By night the streets were thronged with vehi-
cles and foot passengers every one eager to see and hear what was going

on. Many visitors were completely taken by surprise and could hardly reconcile it with their preconceived ideas of our sleepy, old Virginia town; confessing it resembled more a foreign capital in a holiday time than an American city and needed only the "masks and confetti" to complete the picture of an Italian Carnival; so that we feel assured whatever impression the visit to Yorktown made on the temporary sojourner in our midst seeking recreation and pleasure, the memory of the days spent in Norfolk during the last week will always be an agreeable one.

COMMERCE STREET—WATER TO MAIN STREETS.

And now with a few words of friendly admonition to the folks at home, we will take a respectful leave of our kind readers.

Our natural advantages are undeniable as are also the strong evidences of a right spirit which is begining to manifest itself in and among our people and the merited results have been rapid progress in the past few years. But it is not sufficient merely " to hold the fort "—we must keep moving on as the world revolves and it rests with us to decide whether it be backward or forward.

To accomplish the latter we must posess an energy which is persevering, united and tolerant. Persevering, for "eternal vigilance is the price of liberty" and the rule finds no exception in a freedom from commercial vassalage. Though he may have cleared the rapids and the shoals, the strength of the deep water current requires no less skill and determination on the part of the rower to prevent his drifting back into the escaped danger.

United, for without complete union strength will be wanting and the scattered forces of energy be completely wasted. Individual wishes and prejudices must therefore be cheerfully and patriotically sacrificed for the common good.

Tolerant, for while we cordially invite the stranger to come among us and share our labors and rewards of toil, what inducement is there for him to come if we require him to lay aside all his preconceived opinions and cherished notions, the result perhaps of a life time of labor and thought and conform himself entirely to our views?

No; let us lay low the spirit of Procrustes that would fit every man to the bed of our views and opinions and thus gain the double advantage, in heartily welcoming the stranger to our midst, of numerical strength and a healthy interchange of views.

Actuated by these motives and guided by these rules of conduct a brilliant future is secured to us and though this generations of elders and leaders may pass without seeing a fulfilment of our predictions, there are among us youths now on the march of life, who will be found side by side with these bright hopes and will develop our great natural advantages into that majestic grandeur which God intends one day or another to confer upon us.

To those who have glanced over our preliminary sketch or perhaps honored us by giving it a thorough perusal, we would here say please don't lay the book aside, for the subject is by no means exhausted; we have just crossed the threshold and we give you a most hearty welcome to walk in and see what a feast of good things—aye and as useful as good—is spread out before you. We are coming now nearer to the every day life of our busy people, for while we have touched lightly on our City's outer life and connections with the world at large and its great expectations springing up in a bountiful crop therefrom, we still have to show you our peoples business life on her streets and invite you all who may be attracted by our prospective greatness and present prosperity, to come and mingle with us and take hold with us and share with us the profits of our successful business developments. Turn over the leaves of our book and examine each page of it and you will find new matter constantly recuring to interest and instruct you, for we have been at no little expense and pains to present an accurate and thorough list of all the avenues of commerce, manufactories, trades and firms of the city and such general information concerning them as must be most useful to those who already have or who may desire to have business relations with our city.

THE ASSOCIATED RAILWAYS.

IMMIGRATION INTO VIRGINIA, THE CAROLINAS AND
GEORGIA, AND THE LEADING RAILWAYS OF THESE
STATES AS FACTORS FOR MOST SUCCESSFULLY IN-
DUCING IT.

TO argue the advantages of immigration is to presuppose a want of
common intelligence in the readers of this journal. To waste
one's time in inquiring into the reasons why the unproductive hill sides
of New England and the vast stretches of prairie in distant Western
Territories have yielded to the treatment of nature and foreign industry,
and become transformed into a new existence with all that is useful and
beautiful in the realms of commerce, comfort and art, is also a needless
task. We accomplish nothing by such speculations. Dealing, therefore, with the facts as we find them, that the forests of our Southern
lands are, to a great extent, primeval ; that the mineral and metalic
riches of our hills and mountains remain unexhumed ; that our water-
powers of Titanic strength run to the sea almost entirely unarrested in
their course by the demands of commerce or manufacture ; that flocks
of sheep and herds of cattle graze only here and there upon our mead-
ows, and that in all the departments of agriculture, manufacturing and
mining industries around us, undevelopment is the rule and development
the exception, the question recurs, by what appliances and methods
could changes in such conditions be best effected ?

It was only when transportation for man and beast, and the products
of the fields and forests, and the mines became practicable on methods
of uniformity upon and harmony with the leading railways of Virginia
and the Carolinas, and when, with such uniformity and harmony,
economy of cost followed as a consequence to the consumer and producer.

By arrangements entered into in the autumn of 1880, between the leading lines that traversed the South Atlantic States, viz : the Richmond and
Danville Railroad system, the Atlantic Coast Line system, and the Seaboard Air Line system, united tarffic management occurred, competition
among numbers of these lines ceased, uniform methods of rates and
service were created, and it became possible, as a legitimate branch of
the Passenger Service which had, as well as the freight department of
said lines, been concentrated under the control of one officer ; to create
a Bureau of Immigration and Settlement ; to agree with connecting
railway and steamer on rates of inland transportation ; to perfect methods

of ocean transit with Trans-Atlantic Steamer Lines; to offer to the New England, Canadian or Foreign Immigrant the opportunity of being ticketed directly from his present home to any point upon said lines at which he might wish to make a new dwelling place; to collect from all quarters absolute and complete descriptive lists of farms and forest lands, water-powers, mining and manufacturing properties, &c., throughout the territories in the four States that these railways reached, and to distribute such information in all quarters likely to attract the attention of intending settlers; and in fact to create and put in successful operation, even to the minutest detail, a system for the sale or purchase of land and information to the immigrant, the investor or the capitalist, which unites in presenting to their attention whatever exists in the States named that is valuable or attractive, all this has been done.

Foreign agencies have been created; information as to routes and cost of transportation--the character and localities of lands, and all required appliances and facilities for reaching the sections of country, traversed by said lines, have been printed in the language of the country in which this information is distributed and from whence immigration is expected.

The managers of the railways at interest recognize that it is only by patient and persistent effort based upon thoroughly comprehensive plans, that success in developing immigration can be achieved in the territories these lines reach. Therefore it is, that confinement to description of properties of one particular class, or in any one area of territory, is not practiced. Neither do the boundaries of a particular State circumscribe their efforts.

It is with equal exactitude and impartiality of description that the abstracts of land that are published by their Bureau of Immigration embrace the mineral and timber lands of Virginia and Western North Carolina, the tobacco and grain-growing sections of the same States, and likewise the fruit and vegetable-growing localities, also the cotton-producing uplands and lowlands of the Carolinas and Georgia, also the health resorts and wealth of scenery, with which the mountainous sections abound.

It is also contemplated to particularly describe the character, extent and capacity of the water-powers with which all these sections abound, and their adaptability for profitable use, either by the man of limited means with simple machinery, or wealthy companies capable of accomplishing their highest development

Furnishing after this fashion an assortment of the resources and attractions with which these lines abound, it is equally their intention, to which execution is now being given, to reach the various classes of people likely to become interested in these matters. For instance, the Canadian forests or the Scandinavian peasant can find congenial employment in the exhaustless forests of the higher latitudes or cooler climates of the mountainous sections; the Middle and Eastern States farmer, as well as the English or German immigrant, can find in the grain and tobacco growing or grazing lands locations adapted to their ideas and habits, while among the sunny slopes of the uplands of the Piedmont sections, the French and Swiss vine-growers can find homes not unlike those of their native lands; and thus, *ad infinitum*, it is certain that every class appealed to can be offered inducements for seeking locations among us that possess features not unlike those of the homes they leave.

It is with pleasure, therefore, that we invite the attention of our readers and all interested in the material development of our sections, to the advertisement of the Associated Railways of Virginia and the Carolinas that appears in this volume.

A WORLD FAMOUS ESTABLISHMENT.
Valentine's Meat Juice Manufactory.

THE City of Richmond has its Iron Works and its Flour Mills, both of which have gone far to render that city in proportion to its size, one of the leading manufacturing centres of the country—certainly of the South. But she has also one article of manufacture, possessed by no other city in the country; an article which has built up a highly enviable reputation for itself and strictly upon its own merits, not only in this State and throughout the Union but in Canada, Europe, Africa and South America. From the Rocky Mountains to the Pyramids and back again to the Andes, therefore, it may be truthfully said that VALENTINE'S MEAT JUICE has easily won the favorable recognition which was its due. This is evidenced by the medals and diplomas awarded the Proprietor Mr. Mann S. Valentine, one of the most enterprising and pushing citizens of Richmond, by the Philadelphia Centennial of 1876 ; Paris Exposition of 1878 ; and by the International Medical and Sanitary Exposition London, 1881 ; the value of the latter testimonial is particularly worthy of mention, as those awarding it were *connoiseurs* in preparations of this nature and were widely known and representative medical men and sanitary scientists. The MEAT JUICE is made from the flesh of only the healthiest and tenderest beef cattle, by means of specially adapted machinery ; Texan cheap beef is not utilized in the process, it being tough and coarse. About ten thousand pounds of the finest beef are slaughtered daily outside the city for manufacture and the crushed animal fibre is then conveyed to the works and subjected to the various processes necessary to transform it into the pure MEAT JUICE.

The cattle, the flesh of which is used in the manufacture of the MEAT JUICE is obtained from the Western and South-western sections of this State, of the Durham breed, specially selected and averaging in weight 1500 pounds. As illustrating the care and exactness observed in its making, it should be stated that when tested *the specific gravity of the contents of every bottle is the same.* It is almost unnecessary to add that such results can only be obtained by scientific nicety and care in the preparation. An intelligent understanding of the practical value of the MEAT JUICE may be had when it is stated that actual experiments have shown the contents of a two-ounce phial of it to equal one and one half pints of the liquid animal essence which latter will sustain a human being for at least forty-eight hours. VALENTINE'S MEAT JUICE has attained its present widespread popularity solely and simply by virtue of its acknowledged purity and intrinsic value.

To sum up, the experience of large numbers of persons thoroughly qualified to speak intelligently of its good qualities, goes to show that it is easily portable, being always convenient to carry, and on this account being particularly useful when travelling either on sea or land—is not affected in any way by changes of temperature or climate (the trouble with most other preparations of the kind)—and in short furnishes a long sought for and reasonably priced article of food containing the very largest amount of nutriment in the smallest possible compass.

Mr. Valentine will shortly erect new works with entirely new machinery and greatly increased capacity for production and manufacture.

HOTELS.

A STRANGER arriving in Norfolk for the first time is struck with nothing more forcibly than with the elegance and extensiveness of our hotel accommodations. Very often he expects to find here insufficient, inconvenient and uncomfortable suggestions of the provincial town in this important element in a travellers calculations, but he is sure

to discover his mistake as soon as he is once ensconced under the roof of
of our hotels.   This however is only   natural   as in the first place Norfolk is the centre of a region producing the best to be had anywhere in
the way of eating and drinking, and prices are of course reasonable in
proportion to the short distance over which goods have to be brought to
market.   Then, too, the hotel buildings are roomy, commodious, well
ventilated, and conveniently located in the heart of the city where they
are easily accessible to railway depots, steamboat wharves, churches,
places of amusement, stores &c.

In architectural design and fine appearance, both without and within,
they will compare favorably with any hotels in the South.   They possess
handsome parlors, reception rooms and dining halls, and chambers both
single and *en suite;* all are well lighted, and being lofty, well ventilated
and handsomely furnished, have an appearance of cleanliness and general
attractiveness not always found in hotels.   The buildings are heated by
steam and furnished throughout with electric bells, elevators and all
modern conveniences.   Seekers of the health and pleasure, commercial
travellers and many others who constantly visit Norfolk, will testify to
the excellence of our hotels.

NEW ATLANTIC HOTEL!
Cor. MAIN and GRANBY STREETS, NORFOLK, VA.
Terms, $2.50 and $3.00 Per Day, According to Location,

R. S. DODSON, Proprietor.

Enlarged, remodelled and refurnished, rendering it one of the handsomest structures
in the South, possessing all the modern improvements, including first-class passenger
elevator, electric bells, suits of rooms with hot and cold baths.

The especial attention of Tourists and Invalids is called to the fine climate of Norfolk and vicinity, and to the accommodations afforded by the ATLANTIC, where nothing will be left undone to render them comfortable.

☞ Liberal arrangements made with families and parties by the month.

☞ Letters and telegrams to R. S. DODSON, will receive prompt attention.

Hygeia Hotel, Old Point Comfort, Va.

Harrison Phoebus, Proprietor.

Situated one hundred yards from Fort Monroe, at the confluence of the Chesapeake Bay and Hampton Roads, being the first point of land lying westward between the Capes of Virginia, about fifteen miles north of Norfolk and Portsmouth; all passenger steamers running to and from those cities touch at the pier, going and returning, with the U. S. Mails, landing only twenty rods from the Hotel, which is substantially built and comfortably furnished; has hydraulic passenger elevator, gas and electric bells in all rooms; water; rooms for bath, including *Hot Sea*, and closets on every floor, with the most perfect system of drainage of any Hotel or public building in the country. And as a resort for the pleasure-seeker, invalid, or resting-place for tourists on their way to Florida or the North, this house, with accommodations for about seven hundred guests, presents inducements which certainly are not equalled elsewhere as a summer resort or cold weather sanitarium. Has during the cold weather over 6,000 square feet of the spacious verandas (of which there are over 21,000 square feet encircling the house on all sides) incased in glass, enabling the most delicate invalid to enjoy the sunshine and fine water view without risking the slightest exposure. The invigorating atmosphere and mild temperature being especially adapted to that class who seek the genial winters of the South and cool summers of the North. For sleeplessness and nervousness, the delicious tonic of the pure ocean air and the lullaby of the ocean waves rolling upon the sandy beach, but a few feet from the bedroom windows, are most healthful soporifics at the HYGEIA.

For further information, address, by mail or telegraph,

HARRISON PHOEBUS, Proprietor.

PURCELL HOUSE,

NORFOLK, VA.

R. T. JAMES, Proprietor.

Terms, $2.00 and $2.50 Per Day.

This Hotel is conveniently and pleasantly situated, at a short distance from the principal Railroad Depots and Steamboat Landings in the city.

Street Cars pass the door going either way.

House furnished with electric call bells, elevators, hot and cold baths, and every convenience for the comfort of guests.

The House has been remodelled and refurnished until it is second to none in the South in completeness.

The table is supplied with every luxury afforded by this market.

OCEAN VIEW!

THE SEA-SIDE

Summer Resort

OF VIRGINIA.

This delightful and unsurpassed Summer Resort will be open for the accommodation of Guests

ON MAY 1st, 1882.

The location is the most desirable on the South-Atlantic Seaboard, being in full view of Capes Charles and Henry, the Rip-Raps, with un- equalled surf bathing and fishing within a stones throw of the door. The fresh, invigorating breezes render the days delight- fully temperate, while the nights are cool and enjoyable.

The **CUISINE** *includes every luxury of the season, while Guests receive every attention and are provided with every possible comfort.*

The buildings have recently been enlarged and other- wise improved. As a Summer resort it offers unexcelled advantages.

For further information, apply by telegraph or mail to

J. A. KENNEDY, Proprietor,
NORFOLK, VA.

BANKS AND BANKERS.

THE banking facilities of a city may generally according to their limit be considered as forming the best possible index to the financial solidity or weakness of the community in which they are situated. One of the first questions a man who wants to engage in mercantile pursuits in Norfolk or who desires to conduct a commercial acquaintance with our merchants is likely to ask is " How are your banking facilities?" Banks form the great mediums of exchange between countries and commonwealths and not only constitute the bulwarks of trade but offer almost without exception the safest and surest investment for floating capital. The amount of capital invested in Norfolk's banks aggregate very nearly two and one half million of dollars, the basis of transactions the total of which place us as a banking community above many Southern cities of far greater numerical strength. While the sum mentioned may not seem a considerable one yet it is fully equal to all demands of trade upon it and what is more to the purpose money is never so light but what it can be obtained on good commercial paper at reasonable rates.

The increase in the shipment of money into the country by our banks is shown by the statement that in November, 1880 one bank shipped in currency to North Carolina $1,500,000. The greatest stimulous during the year to the banking business is the movement of cotton at this port. The operations of the Clearing House greatly facilitate the prompt and accurate settlement of business. This institution was established in 1871. Its members are the Presidents and cashiers of the following banks in the order in which they are recorded on the books of the Association: Exchange National Bank, John B. Whitehead, President; George M. Bain, Jr., Cashier; Citizens Bank, W. H. Peters, President; Walter H. Doyle, Cashier; Marine Bank, Walter H. Taylor, President; Hugh N. Page, Acting Cashier; Burruss, Son & Co., and the Bank of Portsmouth, Hugh N. Page, Manager, has furnished us with an exhibit of the transactions of the Clearing House during November of each year beginning with

1876	$1,252,675.40
1877	1,117,280.26
1878	1,230,756.26
1879	1,500,925.61
1880	2,024,200.02
1881	2,626,233.68

Particular attention is directed to the gain made during the month of November 1881, and to the fact that this is undoubtedly owing to the generally bettered condition of trade at large in the city. The Savings Banks of Norfolk of which there are several are conducted in each instance on a conservative and judicious policy and greatly assist in the furtherance of the material welfare of the large class of our people, clerks, mechanics, laborers and others who rely for support upon their periodical earnings, and what they are able to lay by therefrom. Wild speculation and commercial gambling are unknown here and it is safe to assume that the monied institutions of Norfolk under their present competent management constitute together the strongest piller in the edifice of our financial weal.

BANK OF COMMERCE.

(Chartered under State Laws, 1st July, 1878.)

DIRECTORS:

JAS. E. BARRY,   D. C. WHITEHURST,   JAS. REID,   SAM'L MARSH,
J. VICKERY,   B. T. BOCKEVER,   R. W. SANTOS,
W. A. GRAVES,   W. S, WILKINSON.

TRANSACTS A GENERAL BANKING BUSINESS. COLLECTIONS MADE ON ALL POINTS AT CURRENT RATES. INTEREST ALLOWED ON DEPOSITS IN SAVINGS DEPARTMENT.

N. Y. Correspondent, NATIONAL PARK BANK; Phila. Correspondent, FIRST NATIONAL BANK; Boston Correspondent, MERCHANTS NATIONAL BANK.

EXCHANGE NATIONAL BANK
OF NORFOLK, VA.

Designated Depository and Financial Agent of the United States.

AUTHORIZED CAPITAL - - - -	$500,000.
PAID IN CAPITAL - - - - -	$300,000.

Hon. JOHN B. WHITEHEAD, President.

JAMES G. BAIN, Vice-President.

GEORGE M. BAIN, Jr., Cashier.

JAMES H. TOOMER, Assistant Cashier.

DIRECTORS.

Hon. JOHN B. WHITEHEAD,   R. T. K. BAIN,   JAMES G. BAIN,
JOHN JAMES,   R. H. McDONALD,   CHAS. JENKINS,
ORLANDO WINDSOR.

STATEMENT OF THE CONDITION OF THE
EXCHANGE NATIONAL BANK,
OF NORFOLK, VA.

At the Close of Business, December 31st, 1881.

RESOURCES.

Loans and Discounts.	$2,281,916	66
United States Bonds	502,300	00
Other Bonds and Stocks	202,504	39
Real Estate, Furniture, &c..	75,336	30
Due from Reserve Agents	421,170	51
Due from other Bks. & Bkrs.	191,576	11
Due from U. S. Treasurer	15,535	35
Specie	130,510	90
Currency	135,300	00
Checks and other Cash Items	52,480	03
	$4,008,630	25

LIABILITIES.

Capital Stock	$300,000	00
Surplus Fund	150,000	00
Undivided Profits	106,309	10
Circulation	270,000	00
Dividends Unpaid	700	00
Due to Bankers and Brokers	369,641	17
Individual Deposits	2,739,960	63
U. S. Deposits	72,019	25
	$4,008,630	35

FURNITURE, CARPETS AND PIANOS.

NORFOLK can justly boast of possessing the largest and handsomest warerooms and stocks in this line to be found south of Philadelphia. The varieties displayed include parlor, drawing-room, chamber, office and school furniture, made from the most exquisitely chiseled rosewood or the common Virginia pine—the most exacting tastes may be satisfied. Among the articles usually found in these houses are also window shades, clocks, mattresses, baby carriages, picture cords, tassels, &c. The firms in the business are liberal and enterprising, and their goods are always purchased direct from the factories. Carpets of every quality and design, from the ordinary American makes to the more elegant and expensive Axminster, constitute an important part of their stock, while mattings and many novel floor coverings can be had in profusion. From the most renowned piano and organ factories of the world these instruments are obtained direct, and are offered with the most absolute guarantees, at the same prices that are obtained at the factory. With $175,000 capital, sales aggregating $450,000 were made in 1881.

During the dull seasons, the heads of our principal firms in this business, visit in person the largest factories of the country and make such selections as, in their experienced judgments, are best adapted to the wants of their particular trade.

North Carolina and Virginia purchasers find Norfolk an excellent and advantageous market in which to make their selections, and each succeeding year brings increased business to our merchants. The sale of pianos and organs has grown of late to be very large, owing, no doubt, to the superiority of the instruments offered, together with scrupulous guarantee of our dealers. Experience has taught our people that it is far wiser, more economical and satisfactory to do business with merchants at home, who are in every sense reliable and responsible, merchants whose reputations are above imputation, and who are always accessible when guarantees are to be made good. Some of the firms in this business are composed of men who are appreciated for their commercial and moral worth, and they are recognized as enterprising, wide-awake, prominent citizens.

FURNITURE, CARPETING AND PIANOS.

S. A. STEVENS & CO.

Cor. Main and Granby Streets.

THE OLDEST FURNITURE HOUSE IN NORFOLK.

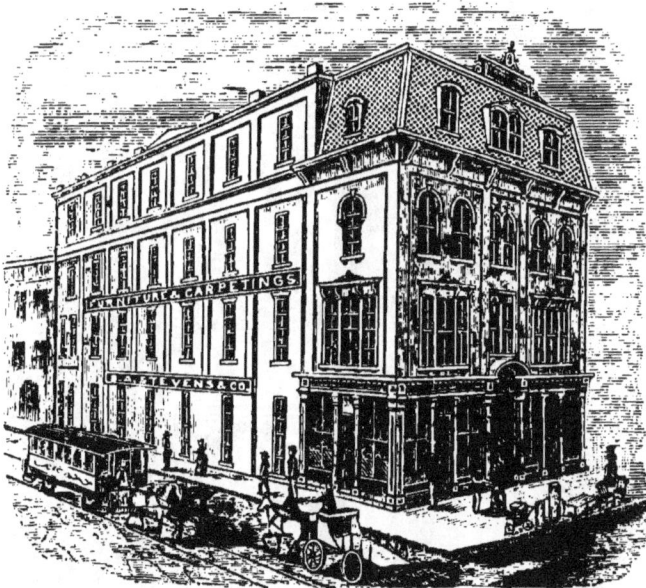

The Largest and Most Complete Stock

OF ANY HOUSE IN OUR BUSINESS IN VIRGINIA.

OUR FURNITURE DEPARTMENT

Is most complete, embracing every article wanted to furnish a house, from the cheapest to the most elaborate and expensive quality.

OUR CARPET BRANCH

Is fully stocked with all grades of floor covering, from that wanted by the poor man for his cottage, to the finest Velvet or Brussels Carpet for the mansion of the rich.

We call especial attention to our **MUSIC DEPARTMENT.** We keep constantly a large assortment of the very best PIANOS made in the World, comprising the celebrated instruments of **CHICKERING & SONS, STEINWAY & SONS, HENRY F. MILLER and W. P. EMERSON.** Every instrument sold at manufacturers' prices and guaranteed for five years.

Our Prices are Guaranteed as Low as in New York or Baltimore.

1865---1882.

THE NORFOLK VIRGINAN.

Cor. MAIN AND COMMERCE STREETS.

PUBLISHED

DAILY AND WEEKLY.

M. GLENNAN, Owner.

NORFOLK, VA.

NEWSPAPER ADVERTISING THE
BEST MEDIUM TO SUCCESS.

————————•————————

Success depends upon the selection of proper mediums and persistency. The best medium, in our judgment, is a good newspaper.—GILLMAN, COLLAMORE & CO.

————————

We have tried almost every medium in advertising and long ago became convinced that the results were largely in favor of newspapers.—IRVIN, BLAKEMAN, TAYLOR & CO.

————————

Advertise largely in first-class newspapers and you are bound to do a trade.—ELRICH & CO.

————————

Of all the methods open to the merchant for advertising his business, an experience of nearly half a century enables us to unhesitatingly declare in favor of the newspaper. It is, without exception, the most economical, persistent, painstaking and successful canvasser any business firm can secure—LORD & TAYLOR.

————————

I have spent thousands of dollars in advertising in all the old and new fangled methods and have long been satisfied that if a man tells the truth in the newspaper, he is sure to get ample return for his money.—J. H. JOHNSON.

————————•————————

ADVERTISE IN THE VIRGINIAN.

THE NORFOLK VIRGINIAN.

The first number of the VIRGINIAN was issued November 21st, 1865, by Messrs. G. A. Sykes & Co. A, M. Keiley, Esq., and Captain James Barron Hope where the Editors, and the late Holt Wilson, Esq., had charge of the Local Department. Col. J. Richard Lewellen was the business manager.

COUNTING ROOM.

The office was then located on Main Street, opposite the Exchange National Bank, now Hoffman's Dyeing Establishment. The prospectus set forth that "apart from the usual features of journalism, we design that the VIRGINIAN should be specially devoted to the advancement of the prosperity of Norfolk and her sister city, and the large section of Virginia whose interests are common with them." Five months after the first issue a change in the ownership and staff occurred, an interest in the paper having been purchased by Col. Lewellen. Capt. Hope and Mr. Wilson retired from the paper, and Col. William E. Cameron, the present Governor of Virginia, assumed the Editorship. Some months afterwards a new company was formed, consisting of Col. J. R. Lewellen, Solomon Hodges, Edward H. Hodges, T. B. Ruffin and J. C. Adkisson, under the firm name of J. R. Lewellen & Co. In November, 1866, Col. Lewellen withdrew in order to take charge of the *Norfolk Journal.* His interest was purchased by the remaining partners and the firm name was changed to S. Hodges & Co., with J. Marshall Hanna as Editor.

In January, 1867, the management of the paper was tendered to M Glennan, Esq., (then only in his twenty-second year) and on the 17th of the month he entered upon the discharge of the duties of the position. The new firm made their purchase of the VIRGINIAN on a capital of FIFTY FIVE DOLLARS, the total amount of spare change in their pockets, and the terms of the agreement were, that the entire purchase money should be paid in two years, in equal weekly instalments, and a failure to meet any one of the payments would be considered a forfeiture and the payments made looked upon as only so much rent. Mr. Hanna retiring from the Editorship after a service of a few months, the position was offered to and accepted by Capt. Hope. In November, 1867, Mr. Glennan purchased an interest in the paper, and on August 1st, 1868, the office was removed to Nos. 56 and 58 Roanoke Avenue, a building errected expressly for the purpose, enlarged quarters being required in order to meet the increased business demands of the paper. On February 9, 1870, Mr. Sol. Hodges disposed of his interest to the other members of the company, and the firm name was changed to Glennan, Ruffin & Co. In the following year Mr. Edward H. Hodges, on account of failing health, sold his interest, and on December 14, 1872, Mr. Glennan purchased the interest of Mr. T. B. Ruffin, and the firm named was changed to Glennan & Adkisson. On 1st October, 1873, Capt. Hope retired from the editorship of the VIRGINIAN, in order to enter upon the same duties of THE LANDMARK, with which paper he was likewise connected in the ownership. The lamented Capt. John Hampden Chamberlayne, one of the ablest and most brilliant journalists of the country, was selected to fill the vacancy. The business of the paper having steadily increased, it was found necessary either to seek new quarters or improve the premises then occupied, and the owners of the property assenting to the latter in consideration of a renewal of the lease, then expiring, for a new term of six years, a new story was added to the building for the special use of the composing room of the newspaper department, the job room occupying the entire second floor. This improvement was completed in the latter part 1873. On 11th of March, 1876 Capt. Chamberlayne retired from the paper, in order to commence the publication of his paper, THE STATE, in Richmond. Capt. John S. Tucker, afterwards Mayor of Norfolk, was tendered and accepted the editorialship. On March 24th, 1876, Mr. J. C. Adkisson disposed of his interest to Mr. Glennan, in consequence of which the latter became sole owner of the paper.

In June, 1878, Mr. Glennan, finding that the increased business of THE VIRGINIAN required more commodious quarters and greater facilities, and at the same time wishing a more central and convenient location, purchased the large and splendidly-built four story brick building on the S E. corner of Main and Commerce Streets, then known as the Goode House. This location is in the very business centre of the city, on the principal thoroughfare, and in the immediate vicinity of the Post Office, banks and banking houses, telegraph offices, &c. Immediate steps were taken to improve it. The entire interior of the building was changed, the lower fronts on Com-

EDITORIAL ROOMS.

merce and Main Streets remodelled by putting in a handsome open front. The two lower floors were divided into stores and offices from which a revenue could be derived, not only to pay the interest on the investment, but also materially assist in reducing the principal. The corner office on the ground floor, was reserved for the counting room of THE VIRGINIAN. The two upper stories were devoted entirely to the mechanical departments of the office. The composing, stereotyping and drying rooms occupying the upper story, and the extensive job room and bindery the third floor. On this floor was also located the editorial rooms and private office, but recently, the increased business demands of the job office and bindery requiring more space, the editorial rooms were removed to the upper story, in order to give the job and bindery departments the entire use of the third floor. In the rear of the main building was errected the press and engine room, and connecting the press room with the composing and job rooms is an elevator used for lowering and hoisting the newspaper and job forms. Every store, office and work room in the building is supplied with water, and water closets for the needs of tenants and employees are place on each floor. Every convenience and improvement for the rapid dispatch of business introduced. Nothing was overlooked that would tend to facilitate work and add to comfort. The purchase and improvements, including the cost of a magnificent press, built expressly for the Virginian and capable of printing two papers at a time, were made at an outly of nearly twenty thousand dollars. On the first of January, 1879, the new quarters were formerly occupied, the entire removal of all the effects from the old office having been made the day previous, without a break in the usual business, and the event was celebrated by the issue of an eight page paper, giving a full record of the local events of the previous year, a history of our municipal government, and a review of the city's trade. The illustrations will give a very accurate idea of The Virginian Building and some of its work rooms. On the 31st of March, 1880, Capt. Tucker retired from the Editorship, which department has since been conducted by Mr. Glennan.

Such in brief is the sketch of the business career of The Virginian. It is a record of successful journalism unparalelled in history of the press of the South. And while its success as a business venture has been recognized, so also has its influence as a leading journal been conceded. In all matters relating the advancement and prosperity of Norfolk its opinions have been respected, and in the advocacy of all measures that tended to develop the great natural resources of Virginia, its record has been most enviable. Its establishment found Norfolk occupying " the least place among the great Atlantic ports." Now Norfolk occupies a proud position and ranks as the second cotton port in the country. Then military rule " foreign to the genius of our government, and utterly incompatible with liberty," held sway in the Commonwealth, now we enjoy the blessings of " Home Rule," and during the last decade Virginia has shown an increase in population of nearly three hundred and fifty thousand. Her vast mineral wealth is being rapidly developed, agriculture is largely and profitably engaged in, railroads are extending in every direction, steamboat lines have been and are being established, and on every hand, and on every side we have evidences of wonderful enterprise, and witness the cheering results of thrift and progress.

During its career, The Virginian has constantly supported the cardinal principles and leading measures of the National Democratic Party, believing the success of that party best calculated to promoted the prosperity of all sections of our common country. It has insisted upon reform in all branches of the public service and economy in the administration of National

5

State and Local Government. It has been a faithful defender of public credit, and has earnestly struggled to preserve the honor of Virginia from being sullied in the slightest by the taint of repudiation. It points with satisfaction to its advocacy of the formation of a Paid Fire Department, the establishment of the City Water Works, the consolidation of the railroads forming the present Norfolk and Western Railroad, the redemption of the Second Congressional District in 1876, and it is with special pride that it alludes to the success that attended its efforts in bringing about a National Celebration of the Centennial of the Surrender of Lord Cornwallis to General George Washington, and the steps taken by Congress for the erection

THE PRESS ROOM.

of the monument voted by the Continental Congress, commemorative of the great victory achieved by the combined armies of America and France, which finished the war of Independence, established the United States of America, and was the crowning epoch of the Revolutionary struggle. In recognition of THE VIRGINIAN's services in this matter, Mr. Glennan was honored by Governor Holliday with the appointment of Commissioner to represent Virginia at the Centennial, and Capt. Tucker was selected by Senator Johnston as the Secretary of the Yorktown Centennial Commission.

In its desire to advance the business and commercial interests of Norfolk, THE VIRGINIAN has spared neither labor or expense, and its efforts in this

respect have elicited and commanded not only words of praise from our
people, but the most favorable comments from the press of the country.
Specially for this purpose it inaugurated the issuing of eight and twelve-page
"special mammoth editions," when ten thousand copies of each were issued
and circulated all over the country. These issues contained the first general
exhibit of the trade and commerce of Norfolk in all its branches. By this
means the outside world was made acquainted with the rapid strides our
city has taken in its onward march. The magnitude of this growth was ex-
plained by tables of statistics, showing with the brevity of figures the kind

THE VIRGINIAN BOOK AND JOB PRINTING ESTABLISHMENT

and quality of business done at this port, and the "issues" contained maps
of the city, with a plan of proposed extension, and of its trade area, exhibit-
ing railroad, steamship and canal lines terminating at Norfolk. They were
also illustrated with views of the city and harbor. The press of the country
compiled statements of Norfolk's trade from these editions of THE VIRGIN-
IAN, and by this means our prosperity was heralded throughout the land.

Such so far has been the work of THE VIRGINIAN. It has not been as
complete as it would wish it, yet it has been as complete as its means and its
labors permitted. But for the kind assistance of a generous public, who
have ever shown their appreciation, it could not have been as successful as
it has been. In the future as in the past it will seek to merit that confidence
and support that has always been extended.

THE VIRGINIAN BOOK AND JOB PRINTING ESTABLISHMENT.

This department of THE VIRGINIAN's business is the most extensive and
complete of any establishment in Eastern Virginian and North Carolina. Its
facilities for turning out work are unexcelled, and we are prepared to exe-

cute every description of job and letter press printing, from a business card to a mammoth poster, with neatness, correctness and dispatch. Fine and color printing is a specialty. Every attention will be given to the printing of books, catalogues, lawyers briefs, letter and note heads, bill heads, shipping tags, business cards, show cards, hand bills, programmes, wedding invitations, railroad and steamboat printing. Large experience in business, the employment of skilled workmen, and the addition of new designs for fancy printing are among the resources of the establishment. Its specimens of printing are always subject to inspection, and all who desire printing are invited to come and judge for themselves. We are prepared to compete with Northern publishing houses, and simply ask and examination and trial.

OUR BINDERY, BLANK-BOOK MANUFACTORY, AND RULING DEPARTMENT.

Besides its job printing Establishment, The Virginian has also an extensive Bindery and Blank Book Manufactory and Paper Ruling Department, by which it is prepared to manufacture, in the best manner and at the shortest notice, all kinds of blank books, such as ledgers, journals, cash and day books, invoice and order books, check and note books, and bills of lading books, in any manner that may be needed, and at figures that will compete with the lowest Northern rates. This department is in the charge of experienced and competent workmen, and we guarantee our work to compete in quality and style with any. Old books rebound, and pamphlets, magazines, music, newspapers, periodicals bound in the best style. By the addition of our Ruling Department we are able to fill all orders for letter heads, bill heads, note heads, railroad and steamboat blanks, and all work of this nature, at reduced rates. Orders solicited and promptly attended to.

Address, "VIRGINIAN," Cor. Main and Commerce Sts. NORFOLK, VA.

JUDICIOUS ADVERTISING
SECURES SUCCESS.

He who invests One Dollar in Business, should invest One Dollar in Advertising that Business.—A. T. STEWART.

Constant and persistent Advertising is a sure prelude to wealth.— STEPHEN GIRARD.

I have most complete faith in printer's ink.   Advertising is the royal road to business.—P. T. BARNUM.

If a man can do Business he should let it be known.—BENJAMIN FRANKLIN.

My success is owing to my liberality in advertising.—ROBERT T. BONNER.

ADVERTISE IN THE VIRGINIAN!

SIC SEMPER TYRANNIS.

WINES AND LIQUORS.

A T no period has the wholesale wine and liquor trade of Norfolk been in better condition than at present. Always large, it has received an impetus in sympathy with other wonderfully growing trades of the city, and while a few years ago only a limited business was done in a limited field, to-day our firms make shipments to the far South and Southwest; indeed, in the Northern States many Norfolk brands of liquors are in demand. Virginia, North Carolina, South Carolina and Georgia have proved excellent markets for our goods, and dealers have not been backward in successfully occupying the field, in competition with dealers of other cities. The purest and richest French, German and native wines, fermented liquors, Bourbon and corn whiskies of the great West are kept in stock, as are also many fancy liquors, of late so popular with those who "smile." The total sales for 1881 amounted to within a fraction of $500,000, divided between firms with a consolidated capital of $150,000.

The retail trade of the city is large, too, the annual scales reaching fully $500,000. German habits and customs, now so common among our people, have succeeded in revolutionizing the retail trade. Light wines, beer, ale, or similar refreshing beverages are now drunk to the partial exclusion of stronger liquors. The retail wine and liquor stores of the city are supplied with every description of goods, those of every clime, quality or vintage, and the most cultivated palate can be suited.

W. F. ALLEN,

WHOLESALE

LIQUOR MERCHANT,

AND DISTILLERS' AGENT,

90 Water Street, NORFOLK, VA.

DEALER IN

Old Corn, Antler, Gaff's Star, Imperial Wedding, Auroro and Gaff's WHISKIES,

RUM, GIN, AND BRANDIES,

ORDERS SOLICITED.

JOHN VERMILLION,
IMPORTER OF
Wines, Cigars, Porter, Ale, &c.,
No. 4 ATLANTIC HOTEL, NORFOLK, VA.

H. R. WOODIS,
DEALER IN
Fine Wines, Liquors and Cigars,
CONDIMENTS, &c.
No. 8 BANK STREET, NORFOLK, VA.

GROCERIES.

THE Grocery jobbing trade commands one of the most important and influential positions of any line of business represented in our mercantile community. During the past year the sales have amounted to $5,000,000, an unprecedented increase over those of former years which the business of the retail establishments also for the same period footed up to between $1,500,000 and $2,000,000.

The gain in volume of traffic in 1881 over that in 1880 was a most gratifying one, the percentage being about 20 per cent. Failures in the business during the period covered have been few and far between ; there are none of any moment to be chronicled, but, on the contrary, we have to record only the constantly growing financial strength of the trade. Some few unimportant embarrassments have been reported, but those have been only of such a nature as was not calculated to affect business or to lower materially the standard of success in the years balance-sheet. The maintenance of these conditions points to a healthy normal condition of affairs, and to the good judgment and discretion which characterize the management of the business in Norfolk and the sagacity of the men by whom it is conducted.

The stocks of groceries usually kept on hand are as a rule of an extensive and varied character and are composed of commodities generally to be found in the largest houses, such as flour, meats, lard, sugars, coffees, teas, syrups, salt, fish, powder, shot, fancy articles, candy &c., &c.

These necessaries besides being sent all over Virginia, North and South Carolina, Georgia and Tenessee, in varying qualities, from a car load to a single box or barrel, are also shipped to every part of the Southern Seaboard. Excellent transportation facilities to and from the great Western Agricultural Mechanical and Commercial centres and constant communication by sail and steam with every principal port at the North and in Europe, there exists no well founded reason why Norfolk should not be able to secure and independently maintain a large share of the Southren grocery trade. The removal of freight discriminations against this city will undoubtedly aid in this development and it is to the deepest interest of our merchants to use their utmost influence toward this end.

It is important for our prosperity that the managers of railroads favorable to the interests of Norfolk should inaugurate a system of prorating upon freight so that freights from here throughout the South shall have the advantage of as cheap rates of carriage as freights from more Northern points. It is safe to assume that when we begin to reap the benefits of this plan our grocery trade will rapidly increase its proportions. One item that bids fair to form a considerable factor in enlarging the grocery trade here, is the direct importation of coffee in vessels which will be able to return with cargoes abtainable from the West, when the transportation facilitates with that section which are now being consummated are finally secured. The approximate amount of capital invested in the grocery business here is $550,000. Total sales $7,000,000.

ESTABLISHED 1871.

E. T. POWELL,   J. R. POWELL.

E. T. POWELL & SON,

(Successors to EASTHAM, POWELL & CO.)

Wholesale Grocers,

90 WATER STREET AND 41 COMMERCE STREET,

NORFOLK, VA,

LARGE DEALERS IN

FLOUR, MEATS, SUGARS,

Coffee, Teas, Syrups, Salt,

Lard, Mackerel, Herring,

AND IN FACT ALL ARTICLES USUALLY KEPT IN A

WHOLESALE GROCERY HOUSE.

Special inducement offered to Prompt Paying and Cash customers.

ESTABLISHED 1871.

E. T. POWELL,   J. R. POWELL.

E. T. POWELL & SON,

(Successors to EASTHAM, POWELL & CO.)

Wholesale Grocers,

90 WATER STREET AND 41 COMMERCE STREET,

NORFOLK, VA.

LARGE DEALERS IN

FLOUR, MEATS, SUGARS,

Coffee, Teas, Syrups, Salt,

Lard, Mackerel, Herring,

AND IN FACT ALL ARTICLES USUALLY KEPT IN A

WHOLESALE GROCERY HOUSE,

Special inducements offered to Prompt Paying and Cash customers.

ESTABLISHED 1865.

M. L. T. DAVIS & CO.,

WHOLESALE

GROCERS,

AND DEALERS IN

Provisions,

FLOUR, FISH & SALT.

CAR-LOAD SALES made a specialty,

AND THE

LOWEST POSSIBLE FREIGHT RATES SECURED.

91 WATER STREET,

(CORNER COMMERCE,)

NORFOLK, VA.

JOHN Z. LOWE,

WHOLESALE AND RERAIL DEALER IN

Fine Family Groceries, Ship Stores, Provisions,

FINE WINES, LIQUORS, CIGARS, TOBACCO, &c., &c.

13 and 15, Corner Market Square and 1, 3 and 5 Union Street,

NORFOLK, VA.

ROASTED COFFEE AND FINE TEAS A SPECIALTY.

FLOUR AND GRIST MILLS.

NORFOLK is without a competitor in the superior quality of flour manufactured by her mills, and their productions find ready sale in our home and foreign markets. The climate of Norfolk being humid, our mills are enabled to produce a better grade of family flour than even those of the more famous milling districts of the State. In Eastern sections of Virginia and North Carolina there are very few mills, and Norfolk supplies the demand of this estensive trade area, it being a well-known fact that the wholesale groceries of the city handle it in such quantities that the mills are never with large stocks on hand, and that our merchants also deal in this specialty to a much greater extent than do those of other business centres with a general trade of the same volume as ours. Our mills also turn out a very superior quality of meal, which is bolted through silk cloths, a process not applied in a great many mills in the South. The mills in this city are built of brick, furnished with the latest and most improved machinery. Combined, they contain thirteen run of burrs, and can produce daily 150 barrels of flour, 850 bushels of bolted meal, and about 200 barrels of hominy. "Old Dominion," and "Purity," are two of the most popular brands manufactured, and they are known to consumers as the the best goods obtainable in this market. With every facility for the cheap delivery of coal at Norfolk, which we are sure will soon be completed, and the advent of grain in large quantities from the far West, the milling interest will undoubtedly take the leading position in our list of manufactures. A few years ago one mill sufficed to stock the market with home-made goods, and even then its success was not fully established, while to-day the two mills referred to are kept going at their maximum capacity.

NORFOLK CITY MILLS

MANUFACTURE ALL GRADES OF

Flour and Meal.

PURCHASERS OF GRAIN

AT ALL TIMES.

LYMAN & CO.,

Hardy's Wharf.   NORFOLK, VA.

SEEDSMEN.

SURROUNDED by such an immense trucking area, it is not at all surprising that the seed business has grown and prospered to the very great extent which it has. Sales are not made exclusively to truckers, however, but shipped from here to almost all parts of the United States, where people desire to cultivate vegetables, flowers, &c., that have found successful propagation in this section. The seedsmen of Norfolk grow most of their seed under their own, or such supervision as will insure the highest state of perfection and vitality. They handle very few fancy seed, but aim specially to produce such as are best adapted to the Southern climate.

The large and substantial patronage enjoyed by dealers in this line, in this city, is sufficient proof that they conduct the business upon the most correct principles. To build up and retain the trade of our truckers from year to year requires the most conscientious, earnest watchfulness, upon the dealer's part, for the purity and reliability of his goods, besides a thorough understanding of the most minute details of the business, even to planting, cultivating, gathering and handling when in stock.

GEORGE TAIT,
SEEDSMAN,
IMPORTER OF AND DEALER IN
ENGLISH, GERMAN, FRENCH CANADIAN AND AMERICAN SEEDS,
No. 7 Market Square, (East Side), Norfolk, Va.

STEAM BAKERIES.

IT may not be amiss at the opening of this brief sketch to remind the reader that Norfolk crackers have gained nearly as favorable a reputation as Norfolk oysters, and that, we consider high praise of one of the principal products of our steam bakeries. In this business Norfolk does a profitable and quite extensive trade. We have here seven bakeries but one only operated by steam and adapted to doing business on a large scale. The local retail trade keeps the smaller establishments generally pretty busy and their wares find their best guarantee in their large consumption in the city. Of course the largest handlers of goods of this kind manufactured here are the wholesale grocers and commission merchants, and this is so to such an extent that it is unusual to find goods manufactured elsewhere ever brought into competition with our own, the former as a rule could not stand it. The marine trade in the products of Norfolk's bakeries has long been very considerable, they being adapted to use in salt air and so made as to resist atmospheric changes. Large shipments of fancy cakes, crackers, &c., are also made to the South. The trade is greatly benefitted by being enabled to purchase its supplies, such as sugar, molasses, flour, &c., right here on the spot and this is productive of obviously good results. The total amount of capital invested in this branch in 1881 amounted to in the neighborhood of $350,000 ; and the prospects for the future are gratifying.

JAMES REID.   W. T. NIMMO.   C. C. REID.

NORFOLK
STEAM BAKERY,

ESTABLISHED 1856.

JAMES REID & CO.,

Manufacturers of all kinds of Superior Excelsior

American Biscuits,

BREAD, CAKES, CRACKERS, &c.

No. 87 Main Street,

NORFOLK, VIRGINIA.

Factory, Holt's Lane and Elizabeth Street.

N. B.—Parties ordering their Goods through their COMMISSION MERCHANTS, will get them at FACTORY PRICES.

DRUGS, PAINTS AND OILS.

THE Showing in this trade is excellent, and although its details are small, the business continues to grow in volume. Both wholesale and retail stores have about them all the appearances of prosperity, and they are pushing trade about as vigorously as it is possible for them to. Last year's transactions represented a money value of $450,000, divided between three wholesale and fourteen retail stores, having in all capital amounting to $150,000. The stocks are large and the stores handsome, the heavier goods being stored in large warehouses, where convenience and safety are matters of paramount importance. Besides Drugs, Paints and Oils, all our wholesale houses carry full lines of Window Glass, Perfumery, Spices, Teas, Champagnes, Wines, &c., and fancy articles of the most beautiful design. The many indigeneous roots and herbs gathered in Virginia and North Carolina are shipped in large quantities from this city. Druggists and country merchants can secure as pure goods and at identically the same prices as can be had in any city in the Union, and in many instances purchases can be made here upon better terms than elsewhere.

BUILDERS' MATERIAL.

SO great has been the advance in this department of trade that the humblest and cheapest dwellings in the city, built during the past few years, far surpass in durability, comfort and ornamentation, many costly edifices of former times. While the character of these buildings has improved, the cost of building has been considerably decreased. The quality of bricks manufactured around Norfolk is good, and the competing yards being numerous, prices have been brought down to their lowest. Fine pressed bricks for fronts are obtained from Philadelphia and Baltimore, Norfolk yards making only rough work.

Dealers in building material in the city occupy large warehouses, some of the largest in the city, and their stocks of finishing Limes, Cement, Plaster, Laths, Press, Cornice, Paving and Building Bricks, are large.

Surrounded by saw mills, Norfolk is an excellent market for Sash, Doors, Blinds, Mouldings, Brackets, &c. Millions of feet of building material of home manufacture find ready purchasers, the quality of the material being good, at regular figures. Contractors find ample stocks for regular goods, and every facility for the prompt execution of their orders at the mills in and around the city.

NORFOLK'S EXPORT TRADE.

THIS is a topic of such extent and such varied interest that it is found almost impossible to do it full justice in the somewhat circumscribed limits to which we are subject. The wonderful and constantly increasing growth of the export trade of the city of Norfolk has been unprecedented in the commercial annuals of any American community. The many doubts and anxieties which encompassed the establishment of the export trade and its subsequent incipient stages but which gradually faded away before its widely broadening influence and stability have at length given place to sentiments of the most thorough confidence in its permanency and importance.

In the accomplishment of this grand result credit should not only be accorded to the efforts of our leading merchants, but the indefatigable efforts of the press of the city and state as well.

The first cotton cargo ever shipped from this to a foreign port was that on board the ill-fated steamer Ephesus, in the Spring of 1866. The Ephesus was wrecked on Sable Island. This might have been considered an ill omen for the future of the export trade, but fortunately its evil influence has not yet been made apparent. The value of the cargo of the Ephesus was $119,023 ; total exports for that year in assorted cargoes $413,405. For the year previous $11,538, all except a few hundred dollars worth of this being in stores. Thenceforth renewed efforts were made to foster a direct foreign trade. In 1874 almost 50,000 bales of cotton were sent abroad, and prospects began to brighten. In 1866 the cotton exports as stated above were valued at $119,023; in 1880 they were $17,508,724. Total in 1866 $413,405—in 1880 $18.005,158, and in 1881 $16,469,570. Comment is unnecessary.

The Seaboard Compress Company operating two compresses ; The Virginia Compress Company operating one compress ; and the Shippers Compress Company operating three Compresses, one in Norfolk and two in Portsmouth are all doing a large business in compressing cotton for direct shipment, and with the advent of another season their facilities will be taxed to the utmost. An ever increasing need at this port is wharf facilities. Last season they were partially inadequate even with the large and elegant wharves errected by the N. & W. R. R. Company. This latter work by the way is a most important improvement and adds several thousand feet to our available water front.

Cattle shipments from southwestern Virginia in 1880 promised to form a considerable factor in our exports, the value of this item shipped to Liverpool that year being $117,100.

The following Tabular Statement will be found of interest :

Exports of Cotton by Bales for 17 Years, from September 1st to August 31st, each Year :

SEASONS.	BALES.	SEASONS.	BALES.
1865-'6	733	1873-'4	20,346
1866-'7	14,168	1874-'5	67,512
1867-'8	8,279	1875-'6	108,683
1868-'9	7,527	1876-'7	116,855
1869-'70	4,745	1877-'8	159,357
1870-'1	5,142	1878-'8	203,536
1871-'2	4,687	1879-'80	257,065
1872-'3	8,282	1880-'1	328,818

DIRECT EXPORTS BY ARTICLES,

FROM JANUARY 1ST, 1865, TO DECEMBER 31ST, 1881, INCLUSIVE.

ARTICLES.	1881.	1880.	1879.	1878.	1877.	1876.	1875.	1874.
Cotton	$16,074,613	$17,509,724	$11,778,181	$9,433,769 00	$5,470,592 91	$7,330,035 00	$5,634,022	$3,239,786
Staves	142,992	167,900	198,900	298,749 21	395,373 36	234,127 00	405,446	373,183
Corn	144,247	122,106	116,395	142,441 00	246,426 00	185,039 00	118,200	7,327
Head Cattle		117,100	67,350	52,630 00	......	......	......	......
Timber	10,062	84,375	45,860	48,000 00	47,709 00	......	......	......
Manganese	50,649	55,141	17,724	12,000 00	......	......	......	......
Shingles	900	1,950	2,343	8,538 75	7,114 12	592 00	6,795	5,609
Flour	125	658	9,652	7,959 00	9,035 00	8,319 00	18,708	7,400
Rosin	......	......	10,499	5,685 00	2,994 00	851 00	290	7,185
Treenails	300	......	......	5,432 00	5,083 00	9,685 00	12,671	4,172
Pork	......	393	......	3,500 00	13,915 00	11,600 00	165	......
Sheep	......	......	1,000	3,285 50	......	......	523	13,779
Tobacco	20,812	2,900	5,920	300 40	62,399 77	7,903 00	......	......
Miscellaneous	24,870	29,835	47,152	6,556 75	18,291 27	33,007 50	54,499	49,617
Total	$16,469,570	$18,095,158	$12,300,976	$10,028,965 61	$6,278,933 43	$7,635,218 50	$6,414,919	$3,709,058
Tonnage	127,774	136,949	112,485	86,273	62,093	65,521	52,211	48,127

TOTAL EXPORTS—1865—1881—17 YEARS—$91,006,235.54.

See next page.

DIRECT EXPORT BY ARTICLES,

From January 1st, 1865, to December 31st, 1881, Inclusive.

(CONTINUED FROM PRECEDING PAGE).

	1865.	1866.	1867.	1868.	1869.	1870.	1871.	1872.	1873.
		$119,023	$1,580,655	$938,223	$882,949	$675,876	$231,819	$433,320	$712,477
		164,140	226,540	376,089	209,293	186,874	325,876	411,638	368,358
	$11,163	1,158	70,073	149,069	70,996	760	37,605	64,216	46,283
		25,860	9,290	415	7,993	.....	.....	.....	.....
		9,183	5,136	11,314	8,768	2,610	14,737	14,983	6,202
		2,606	11,312	9,671	26,115	1,188	3,842	5,628	3,688
		10,137	20,563	54,558	19,978	7,486	2,000	5,658	4,920
						676			470
		566	906	73	.....	1,025	255	604	
		54,790	537,742	178,989	32,707	20,974	575	60	80,421
	375	25,642	51,963	20,748	56,750		13,698	39,613	35,291
	$11,538	$413,405	$2,514,110	$1,739,149	1,315,549	$898,469	$730,377	$975,720	$1,258,120
						12,530	10,398	20,060	30,508

Total Exports—1865—1881—17 Years—$91,006,235.54

WHOLESALE BOOTS AND SHOES.

SOUTHERN and Southwestern buyers have begun to realize the fact that prices here are in many instances identical with those at the factories, and often less, as our dealers buy in large quantities and when the market is dull, while the smaller dealer or the dealer further South, does not make his purchases until the season has fully opened and then in smaller quantities. Thus it is that Norfolk Boot and Shoe Houses obtain all the advantages offered by an advanced market, and can afford to extend more liberal terms to those who buy later and in smaller lots. We have here several wholesale houses, requiring a combined capital of nearly three hundred thousand dollars to conduct them. This amount is in continual activity, and manipulated by men of broad business ideas and sterling integrity—men who are intimately acquainted with the wants of the trade and thoroughly understand their business in its most minute details. Their annual sales are large, and through the agency of a competent corps of traveling salesmen, many thousands of dollars worth of goods are bought by merchants in the South who rarely if ever visit the market.

While Norfolk's principal trade does not extend beyond the Carolinas, through this one branch her reputation has far exceeded the limits marked out by less enterprising and energetic dealers.

Bills bought here are guaranteed duplicates of regular Northern prices, and dealers are cordially invited to satisfy themselves by a personal examination.

SMITH N. BRICKHOUSE & CO.

WHOLESALE

Boots and Shoes,

Cor. Water & Commerce Streets,

NORFOLK, VA.

SALESMEN,

JOHN W. OLD,   T. M. SAUNDERS,   THOMAS OLD,
FRED. FLETCHER.

RAILROAD, STEAMBOAT AND MACHINIST SUPPLIES.

FROM comparatively small beginnings this trade has grown up to be one of the most important in our city. Being cared for and fostered by the hands of pushing, energetic business men who recognize the prominence it should reach in a seaport of Norfolk's growing nature, it has become one of the foremost branches represented here.

Norfolk is naturally the central point of large railroad, milling, steamboat and rapidly enlarging manufacturing interests, and as a result controls a large trade in the business of which we write. In the year 1868 one enterprising firm started out upon this, then, unoccupied field ; now three houses compete in the conduct of a traffic which has been built up altogether since the date mentioned, and which is annually worth many thousands of dollars and covers operations which before that time were not known in our market. Prior to the establishment of the trade here comparatively trifling but intrinsically indispensable bits of machinery were not to be had here for love or money, or at best at exorbitant prices and then under great disadvantages to the purchaser. Almost invariably they had to be ordered from away. This state of things made the market a poor one in every way. All this has fortunately been done away with by the introduction of mechanical skill and what, as it is well named "the life of trade"—competition. Now any quantity or quality of goods of whatever sort or kind can be as readily and as cheaply found in Norfolk as anywhere in the country. This is particularly so of mill supplies with which Norfolk furnishes the constantly increasing demand from Eastern Virginia, North Carolina, &c. As our commerce increases and our marine and railroad interests grow larger this important branch of trade can not fail to do its part in building up the city and making it the central depot of all this section for such commodities.

BOOKS AND STATIONERY.

THE quality and quantity of reading matter in circulation among the people of any community, will be found very accurately to indicate the extent of the intellectuality and refinement of that people. Where there are large public libraries, many and successful book stores, that carry large and well-selected assortments of choice works, there will be found a large percentage of well-informed readers. While all kinds of business here have been pushing vigorously ahead, that of Books and Stationery has in no wise lagged; on the contrary, improvements have been made from time to time until the stores of Norfolk will compare favorably with those of any city the same size. For beautiful selections of costly bound works of fiction, poems, &c., or for School, Law, Medical, Agricultural, Theological, Scientific and miscellaneous Books, to say nothing of the numerous articles, useful and ornamental, denominated fancy articles, our stores are well known. We have two excellent book stores with well-filled shelves, an and examination of their prices will undoubtedly result in keeping at home much of the trade now going from this city to other markets.

UNIVERSITY OF VIRGINIA.

The Session begins on the FIRST OF OCTOBER, and continues until the Thursday before the Fourth day of July ensuing.

The Institution is organized in separate Schools on the Eclectic System, embracing FULL COURSES OF INSTRUCTION IN LITERATURE AND SCIENCE, and in the PROFESSIONS OF LAW, MEDICINE,

ENGINEERING and AGRICULTURE.

THE EXPENSES of the student (except such as enter the practical laboratories) exclusive of the cost of text-books, clothing and pocket money, are from $356 to $391, according to Schools selected ; or, for those who economize by messing, these expenses are from $266 to $300. No charge for tuition to candidates for the ministry unable to meet the expense.

Apply for Catalogues to F. W. PAGE, Secretary, University of Virginia.

JAS. F. HARRISON, M. D., *Chairman of the Faculty.*

NORFOLK COLLEGE FOR YOUNG LADIES.

OFFICERS:—JOHN L. ROPER, President; KADER BIGGS, Vice President; R. H. WYNNE, Secretary; W. S. WILKINSON, Treasurer.

BOARD OF DIRECTORS—Kader Biggs, W. D. Aydlott, E. T. Powell, S. A. Stevens, Luther Sheldon, George W. Dey, Thomas E. Elliott, W. S. Wilkinson, L. Harmanson, C. L. Upshur, George M Bain, A. A McCullough.

FACULTY—Rev. R. M. Saunders, Principal, Professor of Mental and Moral Science. Mrs. M. J. T. Saunders, Modern Languages, Rev. Thomas Hume, Jr., A.M., D.D., Professor of English Language and English Literature. Newton Fitz, Professor of Mathematics. Rev. Thomas Hume, Jr., Professor of Ancient Languages. Rev. R. M. Wynne, Assistant Professor of Latin. Rev. R. M. Saunders, Professor of Physical Sciences. Miss Mary Gable, Rhetoric, Composition and Elocution. Newton Fitz, Professor of Music, Instrumental and Vocal. Anton F. Koerner, Adjunct Professor of Instrumental Music. Miss Lottie Barker, Assistant in Music. Madame Agnes Dias, Art Department, French and German Conversation, Calisthenics and Gymnastics. Miss Virginia W. Hankins, Principal of Preparatory Department. Miss Belle Boykin, Assistant in Preparatory Department. Miss Charlotte Daniel, Lady Manager of Boarding Department. Miss Hull, Lady Manager of Domestic Department.

BOARDING DEPARTMENT FAMILY—Rev. R. M. Saunders, Mrs. M. J. T. Saunders, Madame Agnes Dias, Miss Virginia W. Hankins, Miss Belle Boykin, Miss Lottie Barker, Miss Charlotte Daniel, Lady Manager; Miss Hull, Lady Manager Domestic Department.

BUILDINGS.

The College Building is planned in accordance with the most improved architectural designs, built of brick, and is three stories high. The first and second stories have each three corridors, ten feet wide, extending through the building. There are in all one hundred and thirty-six windows, most of them very large, securing the greatest abundance of light and the most perfect ventilation. In addition to this, ventilators are arranged in the walls of every room There are between twenty and thirty commodious rooms used entirely for school purposes. The whole building is heated by steam, supplied with water from the City Water Works, and every convenience furnished to make pupils as comfortable as they can possibly be in their own homes. The building is arranged to accommodate THREE HUNDRED PUPILS.

THE BOARDING DEPARTMENT BUILDING

Is connected with the College Building, is three stories high, has two broad verandas running its entire length in front, is lighted with gas and heated by steam, and has bath rooms provided with hot and cold water. The bed rooms, opening into corridors extending through the centre of the building, have an abundant supply of light and air, and are handsomely furnished with walnut furniture, marble-top bureaus and washstands, and springs and best hair mattrasses on beds. There are three parlors, one of which is for the special use of the boarding pupils. All the details of management in the boarding department are those of a well ordered family, comfort, convenience and elegance pervading every department of the household.

EDUCATIONAL APPLIANCES.

All the school rooms are supplied with the best modern school furniture. Every needed help to school work is provided—Slate Black Boards, Maps, Charts, Object Teaching Apparatus, Superior Apparatus for illustrating the Physical Sciences, Pianos, Organ, &c., from the best makers. Statuary Pictures, Studies, Models, &c., for the Art Department. Apparatus for the Calisthenium, &c., &c.

COURSE OF STUDY.

There are three departments—the Primary, the Intermediate, and the Collegiate. In these ample provision is made for the thorough instruction in all the studies from the most elementary to the highest. The Board of Directors can conscientiously ask parents, who wish to secure for their daughters a thorough education and culture, to commit them to the care of the teachers who compose the Faculty of the NORFOLK COLLEGE FOR YOUNG LADIES.

For Catalogue, containing full information as to expenses, &c., address

Prof. R. H. WYNNE, Secretary.

FERTILIZERS.

IN the new and sparsely settled West where the land has been under cultivation but a comparatively short time it needs no stimulus to aid in the growth of necessary crops. In the East however it is very different. New ground has been tilled by successive generations and requires periodical and systematic renewing to render it fertile and productive. To such a marked extent is this so, particularly in the soil in this section of the seaboard where the trucking interest is an extensive and growing one, that the status of the most intelligent and successful farmers is we may say in a measure indicated by their choice and use of fertilizers. Being an article easy of adulteration with all kinds of worthless substances, and the profits on an article of this kind when so "doctored" being very great it, is safe to assert that the agriculturalist can not exercise too much caution in procuring his supplies, or if he makes his purchases contrary to the guidings which have followed the use of the best articles for years past, he is likely to find out his error to his cost, and that very soon. The man who buys fertilizers most intelligently is the man who buys knowing exactly the special deficiencies, and therefore the particular requirements of the soil on his farm and what component is needed to produce a certain crop or crops. The most inexperienced farmer need never have cause to regret his use of a fertilizer if he will only be guided in his course by the experience of others and not trust to irresponsible agents and dishonest manufacturers, who, like their goods have no reputation to lose and only thrive by fleecing the unwary.

The efficacy of fertilizers is quite as well known as their use is indisputed. In proof of this it may be stated that in North Carolina and in some portions of this state the use of the scientifically correct proportions of certain chemicals has produced results in forcing the early growth of cotton when it could have been accomplished by no other possible means. Fertilizers prepared from the crude material are now largely employed, their use being on the increase yearly and since 1880 a number of cargoes of German Potash Salts (Kainit) have been received here by direct importation for local manufacturing purposes. There are two incorporated companies doing business in or near Norfolk which are engaged in the manufacture of fertilizers on a large scale, one having been incorporated as recently as the 21st of March of this year—and this latter fact may be alluded to incidentally as showing the dimensions which this branch of industry is assuming, and its importance to our business interest, particularly the trucking and cotton interests. There are also two large and prosperous firms engaged in the business.

These establishments are controlled by men possessed of capital and energy, and there is no estimating the limits to which the trade will be pushed in the course of the next five years.

In our warehouses may be found Peruvian Guano of direct Government importation, Bone-dust, Animal Matter, Dried Blood, Bone Black, Dissolved Bone, Fish Guano, Plaster, Kainit and the various salts of Ammonia, Soda, and Potash all in good condition, together with other valuable fertilizers. These goods can be bought in Norfolk as cheaply as anywhere else and the quality will not suffer by comparison. Within the last decade progress in this business in Norfolk has been wonderful, and the secret of it has been that our dealers have had the honesty and the good sense to put only such wares on the market as were found to win for themselves only an enviable reputation among all classes of customers.

PEANUTS.

THE peanut might almost be called a Virginia staple product. That the term would be a just one is evidenced by the fact that the peanut raised on Virginia soil is always most sought for in the market and invariably brings the highest prices—and we produce more in this State than in any other where the nut is grown at all. The Virginia nut will sell at from one to one and a half more cents per pound than the Tennessee or Carolina nut. It frequently happens however that competition with inferior grades raised in Georgia and lower Tennessee has lowered the prices of the Virginia product. As the best is coming to be more widely known, however, the injurious results of cutting in prices will disappear, and Virginia planters will find more ample returns than heretofore.

The business in Norfolk is one of by no means inconsiderable proportions. In fact it constitutes one of our chief industries and gives employment to a large number of hands. The demand for the nut increases year by year, and with it increases our facilities for putting it into proper shape for consumption. The season opens in September, though the crop is not harvested until October, except in this State. Virginia furnishes in the neighborhood of sixty per cent. of the crop of the interior United States, while Tennessee produces about thirty-five per cent. In 1880 the entire crop of the country was valued at $2,150,000, of this, Virginia supplied 1,350,000 bushels, Tennessee 750,000 and North Carolina 125,000. The crops of this State and of North Carolina are shipped principally to Northern and North Eastern markets, while those raised in the other Southern States are nearly all sent West.

The whole of tide-water Virginia is a great peanut producing section. The counties in which the cultivation of the much prized product is most extensively entered into are those of Nansemond, Isle of Wight, Surry, Southampton, Prince George and Sussex. Of late years however, the peninsula counties have gone into raising the peanut, and although Warwick was formerly the only county growing it to any extent, it is now under cultivation on many farms in the counties of Elizabeth City and York, and to a lesser degree in Matthews and Gloucester counties. A few are also raised in Norfolk and Princess Anne counties. In 1880 the entire crop of this State amounted to 1,350,000 bushels, and of this quantity Norfolk handled upwards of seventy-five per cent, or in the neighborhood of 1,000,000 bushels. The average price per pound being four and one half cents or ninety nine cents per bushel, of twenty-two pounds. Showing that the amount of capital put into circulation by the peanut in Norfolk in 1880 approximated $1,000,000. The following comparative statements of each year's crop in Virginia from 1867 to 1880 inclusive will be found of interest:

1867	75,000 bushels.	1874	350,000 bushels.
1868	150,000 "	1875	450,000 "
1869	424,000 "	1876	780,000 "
1870	270,000 "	1877	405,000 "
1871	195 450 "	1878	875,000 "
1872	324,000 "	1879	1,000,000 "
1873	225,000 "	1880	1,350,000 "
		1881	750,000 "

From the above table it will be seen that in 1881 the Virginian crop fell off between 40 and 50 per cent. from the crop of the previous year. In 1880 Tennessee produced 750,000 bushels, and in 1881 only 250,000. These deficits are chiefly attributed to the severe and prolonged drouths of last year.

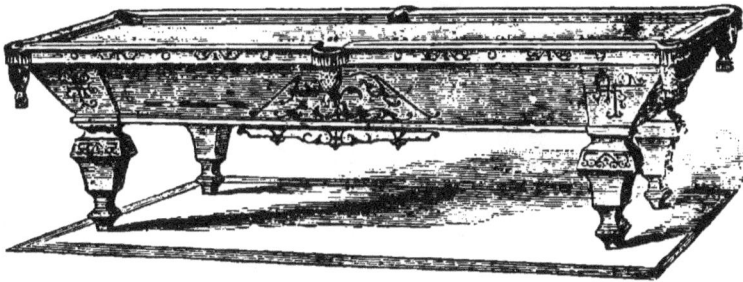

IRON WORKS AND MARINE RAILWAYS.

AMONG the essentially important features of a prosperous commercial sea-port, and too, which are likely always to stand prominent
in our city, are Iron Works and Marine Railways; departments of industry which we may safely say do more directly to further agricultural,
manufacturing and shipping interests than can well be estimated.

Norfolk has four large Merchant Machine Shops, five Foundries and
five Marine Railways. It will thus be seen that we are not lacking in
superior facilities in these branches. We are also so fortunate as to possess sufficient business demand to furnish steady employment for every
iron worker, boiler maker and ship carpenter in the two cities ; there
being almost constantly so much work on hand, that workman who are
able to command good wages in any foundry or ship-yard in the country,
have oftentimes to be sent for from elsewhere.

During every month of the year, but more noticeably while the "boom"
of the busy Winter season is enveloping our city in its golden cloud; the
Iron Works and the Marine Railways of Norfolk are busy. At almost
any hour of the day—and we had almost said of night—can be heard the
clang of the boilermakers mallet, the hammering of the mechanic at the
anvil or the grinding of the chains as some stately craft floats from the

ways in to her native element, fresh from the skillful hands that fashioned her stout parts, or from those of the machinist whose toil planned and executed the throbbing engine that transforms her into a thing of life.

In times of financial depression no elements of industrial employment so lag behind or exhibit so unmistakeably the blighting results of the influences to which they may chance to be subjected as do those branches to which we are alluding. The working classes, the representatives of skilled labor, one of the mainstays of the prosperity of any community, being forced to unwilling idleness, the injurious effect becomes at once apparent throughout the whole body commercial. Fortunately the converse is no less true. Money is largely kept in circulation by those who are paid off daily, weekly or monthly, and when these are steadily employed at fair wages, which, as we have before remarked, is generally the case here with those to whom we more particularly refer, the healthful leaven is sure to exert a highly beneficial influence throughout the whole lump. Such is the demand upon the capacity of our Marine Railways that frequently a vessel is compelled to remain for days or sometimes weeks in the harbor before she can be hauled upon the ways for repairs. Boilers of the very best material and of a workmanship challenging the best of Northern skill, agricultural engines of all kinds, stationery engines and narrow gauge locomotives are all built here. The large proportion of these manufactures are shipped to various points in the South, principally to the cotton and timber districts, invariably giving satisfaction and in many cases securing valuable premiums over all competitors. When we take into consideration what has been done, and what the future is bound to develop, the friends of Norfolk will concede that she has on these scores no cause for any sentiments other than those of pride and gratification.

JAMES POWER & CO.

Iron Yard and Metal House,

DEALERS IN ALL KINDS OF

SCRAP IRON, OLD METAL AND PAPER STOCK.

ALSO, NEW and SECOND-HAND ANCHORS, CHAINS and MACHINERY of all Descriptions.

RETAIL DEPARTMENT CORNER WATER AND CHURCH STREETS,

Wholesale Department 26 and 28 Rowland's Wharf, foot of Rothery's Lane, Norfolk, Va.

WE ARE ALWAYS IN THE MARKET FOR THE PURCHASE OF

OLD WRECKS, STEAMERS, VESSELS, OLD MILLS, &c.

Machinery of all kinds, new and second-hand, bought and sold.

WHITE BRONZE MONUMENTS,

HEADMARKS, STATUARY, PORTRAIT BUSTS

AND

MEDALLION PORTRAITS.

The undersigned respectfully invite all who may be seeking a PERMA-
NENT Memorial (either Monument or Headmark) for departed friends,
to call and inspect our chaste and beautiful designs (over three hundred
in number) of WHITE BRONZE, a material that WILL NOT CRACK,
CRUMBLE OR DECAY; will not DISCOLOR or become MOSS COVERED, but is
known to have stood constant exposure
for the past THREE HUNDRED YEARS,
and has been endorsed and recommended
by the leading Scientists of the world.
It is identical in nature and equal in
strength and durability to the DARK
BRONZE of antiquity. IT DOES NOT
PARTAKE OF THE NATURE OF IRON IN
ANY DEGREE WHATEVER.

A beautiful specimen of White Bronze
Monument and Statuary can be seen in
Elmwood Cemetery, third alley east,
erected for Mr. John R. Ludlow, executor
of the estate of the late Mrs. Elizabeth
Benson.

Our many designs of Wrought and
Cast Iron Railings, painted or galvanized
cresting, iron verandas, weather vanes,
vases, chairs, settees, window guards, and
all kinds of ornamental WIRE WORK. All kinds of light and heavy forging,
done with neatness and dispatch, and at prices to suit the times.

We make a specialty of furnishing the PATENT COMBINATION WROUGHT
IRON RAILINGS, suitable for cemeteries or buildings. This railing is durable, beautiful in design and cheaper than any other for many reasons.

Designs can be seen upon application.

BUTT & CO.,
No. 131 WATER STREET.

RICHMOND
THRESHER, SEPARATOR AND CLEANER,

LIGHT DRAFT,
LOW PRICE.

Threshes Rapidly,
Cleans Perfectly.

Satisfaction
Guaranteed.

Send for
Special Circular.

THE SIMPLEST THRESHER IN THE MARKET.

H. M. SMITH & CO., Patentees and Manf'rs.
RICHMOND, VA.

N. B.—We manufacture in addition to the above a large variety of Implements of all kinds for the farm, and carry the largest stock south of New York. In our list will be found Steam Engines, Saw and Grist Mills, Reapers and Mowers, Plows and Cultivators, Wheel Rakes and Hay Feeders, Cotton Gins and Presses, Farm and Freight Wagons, Spring Wagons, and in fact every Implement and Vehicle needed on a farm. Our Catalogue of 200 pages will be sent to all who contemplate buying goods in our line, whether for sale or use.

Farmers needing Implements or Machines of any kind will find in our Catalogue just what they want, with cuts, discriptions and price list.

Address, P. O. Box, 8.

H. M. SMITH & CO.,
RICHMOND, VA.

ELIZABETH IRON WORKS,

CHAS. W. PETTIT,

PROPRIETOR,

Nos. 280 and 282 Water Street,

NORFOLK, VA.

Manufacturer of Steam Engines, Boilers,

SAW AND GRIST MILLS,

SHAFTING, PULLEYS, HANGERS, FORGINGS AND CASTINGS.

Special attention given to the repair of STEAMBOATS and MACHINERY of all kinds.

☞ MACHINISTS AND BOILER MAKERS sent to any part of the Country to repair work.

STAVES.

THAT Norfolk should have been for many years past a stave mart of importance is not remarkable. Geographical position, nearness to the great stave getting regions of this State, and North Carolina, have made Norfolk a central and convenient point for the shipment of staves, particularly to the West Indies where in fact the large proportion of them find their way to be utilized in the manufacture of barrels and casks for sugar, molasses, rum, &c. For these purposes Norfolk staves are always chosen, and they are also much sought after by Mediterranean grape growers, it being held that the wood of staves from this locality injures the delicate flavor of the wine less than is the case with those from elsewhere. Our staves are carefully cut and they are also subjected to an inspection by regular licensed inspectors, who throw out all not coming up to the standard. In illustration of the growth of the export trade here it may be stated that it amounted to $4,496,641 from January, 1865 to December 31st, 1881. The largest shipments valued at $411,638 were made in 1872.

White oak timber grown in this section is highly esteemed for use in ship building, and on account of its fine grain and toughness has always been in demand particularly by the Navy Department, while it is a matter of record that naval vessels built since the repeal of the measure requiring them to be of white oak, grown within fifty miles of salt water, have compaired favorably in durability to those built prior to the enactment.

For the information and guidance of those engaged in the trade, we re-publish from last year's book the

DIMENSIONS OF AND DIRECTIONS FOR GETTING DRESSED STAVES AND HEADING FOR THE NORFOLK MARKET.

White Oak Pipe staves—54 to 56 inches long, not less than 54 inches.—3½ inches and upward wide; must not be less than 3½ inches, and not less than 1 inch thick on thin edge. White Oak Hhd. Staves—42 to 44 inches long, not less than 42 inches—3½ inches and upward wide; must not be less than 3½ inches, and not less than ¾ inch thick on thin edge. White Oak Heading—28, 30 and 32 inches long—5 inches and upward wide; not less than 5 inches, and full ¾ inch thick on thin edge. White Oak Barrell Staves—32 and 34 inches long, 3 inches and upward wide; not less than 3 inches, and not less than ¾ inch thick on thin edge. Red Oak Hhd. Staves—42 to 44 inches long, not less than 42 inches—should be 4 inches and upward wide; must not be less than 3½ inches in any part, and from ¾ to 1 inch and upward thick on the thin edge. All Staves and Heading must be of sound wood, free from knots and all other defects. Must be rived with the grain, and split from the bark to the centre—not slabbed off. They must be straight, with square edges, and moderately dressed with drawing knife to nearly a uniform thickness. White Oak staves and Heading must be free of sap. Red Oak Staves may have sap on them. White Oaks with sap on them are classed Red Oaks. Makers of Staves should get none less than full one inch thick, to allow for shrinkage in seasoning, and they should lay off the logs one or two inches longer than the Staves are required to be, to allow for the "running of the saw." Want of length is fatal to any of the classes of Staves. All Staves are sold here by the long thousand of 1200 pieces.

The Stave trade of Norfolk is carried on by a few firms of enterprise and wealth and the prospects are, that when the manifold advantages of this port became more generally known this branch of the shipping interest will continue to advance.

WM. H. PETERS.   WASHINGTON REED.

PETERS & REED,

SHIPPING AND GENERAL

COMMISSION

MERCHANTS,

AND DEALERS IN

Staves and Lumber,

Main Street, NORFOLK, VA.

AND

Water Street, PORTSMOUTH, VA.

THE UNITED STATES
MERCANTILE REPORTING AND COLLECTION ASSOCIATION,
HOME OFFICE, 335 BROADWAY NEW YORK,
BRANCHES IN ALL THE PRINCIPAL CITIES.
W. G. JONES, SECRETARY AND MANAGER.

The latest and most improved system of Reporting and Collecting, now in use Organized and supported by the largest Importing, Manufacturing and Jobbing Houses of New York City. Over 8,000 Attorneys and Banks compose the Association.

COAL, WOOD AND ICE DEALERS.

THE great piles of coal seen towering above the limits of the many bins in the coal yards of this city, must impress observers with the fact that its handling requires the employment of a great many people and a large amount of money. All along the water front these yards are located, and vessels are loaded or discharged at very small cost and with little trouble. The immense coal beds situated along the Chesapeake and Ohio Railroad, supply a greater part of the demands of this market, while Maryland and Pennsylvania furnish an immense amount. The great ocean steamers leaving this port carry with them well filled bunkers from our yards, and daily shipments are made to consumers and dealers in Virginia and North Carolina, at points upon streams tributary to the Elizabeth river and the sounds. The seven largest firms in the coal trade do an annual business of $500,000 in coals alone, to say nothing of the sales of wood, which many of them handle in quantities, exclusive of business done by the eleven wood yards. The estimated capital employed by these houses is placed at the modest sum of $100,000. During the Winter season, when this business is at its height, our wood wharves present a most animated appearance, the docks being filled with loaded lighters and the streets with venders anxious for a customer. Machinery for cutting and splitting is to be found in nearly all the yards, and from their continuel motion it may be safely concluded that business is good.

The wholesale and retail ice business of the City is also very large, there being two firms in the business, each having immense ice houses, and they ship large quantities to the fisheries of North Carolina, as well as to other points south of Norfolk.

COTTON AND COMMISSION.

THIS is above all others the great business of our city, and largely to the vigor and enterprise of the men engaged in it, is due the steady growth of Norfolk to the rank which she now holds as the third cotton port of the country, and one of the leading commercial centres on the Southern Atlantic Seaboard. Every year millions of dollars worth of the snowy staple pass through this market, and some of the wealth, which every bale brings, stays here to enrich our merchants and laboring men. At almost any time of the year, particularly in the winter months, the lower part of the city or what is known as " Town Point" is scarcely passable for the immense quantities of cotton stored there. Storage room it may therefore be imagined is hard to find, and this is undoubtedly the case, but owners of real estate and local capitalists generally are beginning to understand that they cannot possibly find a better field of investment than in the building of large roomy and much needed storage warehouses. There are already many warehouses of this description here, but these are not sufficient for the constantly increasing demands of the cotton trade. One or two more seasons will not pass however without affording us an opportunity to chronicle extensive improvements in this respect.

Up to the year 1865 little or no cotton ever came to Norfolk, and the city had no pretensions to the dignity of a cotton port. Since that period every year has added to her importance as a cotton shipping point, until at the present time it is found difficult for the presses owned and operated by the three compress companies of this city to compress and load the cotton fast enough to avoid the blockade, which is sure to result if work is stopped night or day. Heavy draught iron steamers principally British, and sailing vessels of all nations lie, four and five abreast at our wharves during the cotton season loading or waiting their turn to load and start upon their voyages. The cotton is compressed to one third the size in which it comes from the gin and is then stowed for shipment by skilled cotton screwers.

As mentioned incidentally above there are three cotton compressing companies transacting business here. These are the Seaboard, The Virginia and the Shippers Compress Companies. The total capital operated by these establishments is very large, and the respective managements of the compresses are in the hands of men of experience and capacity. The Seaboard Company controls two presses, both at Town

Point; the Shipper's company has one press in Norfolk and one in Portsmouth. All are equipped with the very latest and most improved and powerful machinery, and the three companies have facilities for delivering daily into the holds of foreign bound vessels of all nationalities hundreds of compressed bales of the fleecy staple. The three corporations mentioned, besides conducting the business of compressing, are extensive charterers and shippers on their own accounts and thereby are largely instrumental in augmenting the importance of Norfolk as a cotton port. The following table exhibits the receipts of cotton by bales at Norfolk for 22 years, beginning with September 1st, and ending with August 31st of each year :

Year.	Bales.	Year.	Bales
1858-'9 - - - -	6,174	1871-'2 - - - -	258,730
1859-'60 - - - -	17,777	1872-'3 - - - -	405,413
1860-'1 - - - -	33,193	1873-'4 - - - -	472,446
[War between the States).		1874-'5 - - - -	393,672
1865-'6 - - - -	59,096	1875-'6 - - - -	469,998
1866-'7 - - - -	126,287	1876-'7 - - - -	509,612
1867-'8 - - - -	155,591	1877-'8 - - - -	430,557
1868-'9 - - - -	164,789	1878-'9 - - - -	443,285
1869-'70 - - - -	178,352	1879-'80 - - - -	597,086
1870-'1 - - - -	302,930	1880-'81 - - - -	713,026

The growth of the market has been steady, and the result of causes which have combined to render it permanent.

The following is a statement of receipts and shipments of cotton as recorded at the Exchange :

SEASON 1874-'5—Receipts year ending 31st August, 1875   -   -   -   393,672
    Shipments, coastwise   -   -   -   -   326,281
    Exported Great Britain -   -   -   63,629
    Exported Continent   -   -   -   3,583
    Exports   -   -   -   -   -   67,212
                Total shipments   -   -   -   393 493

SEASON 1875-'6—Receipts year ending 31st of August, 1876   -   -   -   469,963
    Shipments coastwise   -   -   -   -   361,053
    Exported Great Britain   -   -   103,869
    Exported France,   -   -   -   -   1,817
    Exported Continent   -   -   -   3,007   108,693
                Total shipments   -   -   -   -   469,746

SEASON 1876-'7—Receipt year ending 31st August, 1877   -   -   -   509,612
    Shipments coastwise   -   -   -   -   391,838
    Exported Great Britain   -   -   -   112,245
    Exported France   -   -   -   -   1,602
    Exported Continent   -   -   -   -   3,008   116,855
                Total shipments   -   -   -   -   508,693

SEASON 1877-8—Receipts year ending August 31, 1878   -   -   -   430,557
    Shipments coastwise   -   -   -   271,144
    Exported Great Britain -   -   -   -   157,153
    Exported France -   -   -   -   2,204   159,357
                Total shipments   -   -   -   -   430,501

SEASON 1878-'9—Receipts year ending 31 August, 1879   -   -   -   443,285
    Shipments coastwise   -   -   -   -   -   239,158
    Exported Great Britain   -   -   -   199,815
    Exported France   -   -   -   -   713
    Exported Continent   -   -   -   -   3,008   203,536

    Total shipments   -   -   -   -   -   -   442,694
SEASON 1879-'80—Receipts ending 31 August, 1880   -   -   -   597,086
    Shipments coastwise   -   -   -   -   337,226
    Exported Great Britain   -   -   246,674
    Exported France   -   -   -   1,479
    Exported Continent   -   -   -   8,912
    Total Exports   -   -   -   -   -   257,065

    Total shipments   -   -   -   -   594,291
SEASON 1880-'1—Receipts ending 31 August 1881   -   -   -   -   713,026
    Shipments coastwise   -   -   -   -   392,079
    Exported Great Britain   -   -   -   -   216,046
    Exported France   -   -   -   -   -   2,850
    Continent   -   -   -   -   -   -   9,922

    Total Shipments   -   -   -   -   720,887

U. S. Senator John W. Johnston, of Virginia, has within the last two years made an interesting compilation of statistics based on data obtained from official sources, and showing the following comparison between the rate of increase and decrease in the cotton business of the eight largest cotton ports of the country, between the six years ending August 31st, 1861, and a similar period ending August 31st, 1879:

MARKET.							RATE.
Galveston	-	-	-	-	-	-	Increase 197 per ct.
New Orleans	-	-	-	-	-	-	Decrease 28 per ct.
Mobile	-	-	-	-	-	-	Decrease 43 per ct.
Savannah	-	-	-	-	-	-	Increase 44 per ct.
Wilmington, N. C.	-	-	-	-	-	-	Increase 222 per ct.
Charleston	-	-	-	-	-	-	Increase 3½ per ct.
Apalachicola	-	-	-	-	-	-	Decrease 83 per ct.
NORFOLK	-	-	-	-	-	-	INCREASE 1,212 per ct.

Upon examination the table of direct exports for seventeen years on pages, 85 and 86 and it will be seen that from January 1st, to December 31, 1866, 733 bales of cotton valued at only $119,023 were exported. The cotton export value in 1880 amounted to $17,508,724, and in 1881 to $16,074,613, the total value of exported cotton for the seventeen years amounting to $82,044,063.91, with an increase for 1881 over 1866 of $15,955,590 of 1880 over 1866 of $17,389 791.

The completion of numerous railroad connections and the effecting of consolidations favorable to the growing commerce of Norfolk, all of which are alluded to elsewhere in this volume, will it is hoped and confidently believed, greatly augment our cotton receipts and shipments, and also have the further result of impressing upon real estate owners the urgent necessity for more wharf room for the storage of the great bulk of cotton which every season finds its way to our limits. The Norfolk and Portsmouth Cotton Exchange, an institution chartered in 1874 by authority of the Legislature of the State of Virginia, has been a powerful factor in building up our cotton trade. The Exchange is situated on Water Street, easily accessable to the centres of business of which it is in fact the systematic and well governed head. The actual cash capital employed in the cotton commission business in the two cities (Norfolk and Portsmouth) is roundly estimated at $2,000,000 and the commission houses, as well as the regular cotton factories, handle large quantities of the staple and in many instances are represented on 'change.

S. F. PEARCE.   W. F. ALLEN.   J. T. BORUM.

PEARCE, ALLEN & BORUM,

COTTON FACTORS,

AND

General Commission Merchants

20 and 22 Commerce Street.

NORFOLK, VA.

SPECIAL ATTENTION TO THE SALE OF

Cotton, Grain, Lumber, Peanuts, Peas and all other Country Products.

W. W. GWATHMEY.   C. G. ELLIOTT.   TEMPLE GWATHMEY.

W. W. GWATHMEY & CO.,

COTTON FACTORS, GENERAL COMMISSION MERCHANTS,

AND

BONDED WAREHOUSEMEN,

Town Point,   -   NORFOLK, VA.

Largest Warehouse in the City, at wharf of Liverpool Steamers. Norfolk and Western Railroad track at door. Freight by Seaboard Road Delivered free of charge.

ADVANCES ON CONSIGNMENTS.

STEAMBOAT AND STEAMSHIP LINES

THE different railway lines, canals and other avenues of trade and commerce have been fully reviewed in another part of this work, and it is our purpose now to call the reader's attention to the principal steamboat and steamship lines regularly entering this port from the many trade centres of the country. Centuries ago Norfolk became noted for its many and extensive lines of vessels, especially in connection with the foreign trade, but the wealthy and enterprising ship owners of those days little imagined that their crafts would be so soon superseded by the superb iron vessels of to-day. Steam navigation has been adopted on all coast and inland lines and in fact on all regular lines where dispatch is a desideratum; sailing vessels carrying only such freights as are too bulky and difficult to handle, or which pay insufficient freight. Immediately after the resumption of business in 1865, a few steamers, of indifferent construction and limited capacity, were put upon our waters, but as trade grew and the demand for increased facilities became more imperative, changes were made, larger, finer and greatly improved vessels for passenger and freight traffic were from time to time put on, and the old ones withdrawn, for use at points where their accommodations were adopted to all requirements.

To minutely and fittingly describe the different lines now centering here, the unsurpassed splendor of the vessels employed, or to give even a brief notice of the enterprising and wealthy corporations owning them, would require the services of a writer gifted with extraordinary descriptive powers. Suffice it to say that the management of these lines is in the hands of men who appreciate the wants of trade, and with undoubted ability in the conduct of the transportation business, they have estab-

ERRATA.

In W. W. GWATHMEY & CO.'S advertisement, page 122, read, LICENSED Warehousemen, instead of Bonded Warehousemen, and freight by Seaboard Road delivered free of CARTAGE, instead of CHARGE.

Sounds and Rivers of the Old North State, and also to Hampton, Old Point, Fortress Monroe, Smithfield, Cherrystone, Yorktown and Matthews. The fleet comprises about twenty-five iron and wooden vessels aggregating over twenty thousand tons burthen.

The Company was started in 1867, succeeding the old New York and Virginia Steamship Company, and it has gradually grown to its present proportions as a great corporation, with interests and connections in every State in the South and West.

The distance between New York and Norfolk is 285 nautical miles, and the steamers of this line generally make the trip in twenty-five hours. The regularity with which these vessels arrive may be illustrated by an incident which occurred several years ago. The writer was in company with a number of gentlemen when the loud report of a cannon was heard, and he remarked to one of the bystanders that he was not aware of the lateness of the hour, but that the Navy Yard gun had just announced the time of sunset. The bystander replied that the gun fired was not at the Navy Yard, but upon the forward deck of the New York steamer, and added with considerable fervor, "but she's just as regular."

The passenger accommodations of the Old Dominion steamships, are of the most comfortable and superb character; the saloons are substantially and elegantly furnished, the tables well supplied, and in fact they are wanting in nothing calculated to make a trip upon them desirable and pleasant. During the Company's career of fifteen years *not a single life entrusted to its care has been lost.* Through the worst storms and series of marine disasters these steamships have always passed in perfect safety. When the largest of them steam up the river they look as though they were conscious of their beauty, and under the skillful management of their officers, glide quickly but majestically into their docks, there to be relieved of their immense cargoes.

The parent offices of the Company are at 197 Greenwich Street, New York city. The principal officers are: Commodore N. L. McCready, President; W. H. Stanford, Secretary, and H. A. Bourne, Superintendent. In Norfolk Messrs. Culpepper & Turner represent the Company's interests, with their office on the extensive wharf property on Water Street, immediately at the foot of Church Street. In every department of the Company's business experience and efficiency are the stepping-stones to preferment

The principal steamers of the Company, their names, character, tonage, route, &c., are :

The ROANOKE, iron propellor, freight and passengers, 2,354 tons, Geo. W. Couch, master; the finest and handsomest ocean steamship ever floated in this harbor. She arrived in Norfolk on her first trip Thursday, April 6th; runs between New York, Norfolk, City Point and Richmond.

The GUYANDOTTE, iron propellor of the same class and build as the Roanoke, is now being built and will probably go on the line between New York, Norfolk and Richmond, about May, 15th, of the present year.

The OLD DOMINION, iron side-wheel steamship, freight and passengers, 2,222 tons, G. M. Walker, master; New York, Norfolk, City Point and Richmond.

The WYANOKE, iron side-wheel steamship, freight and passengers, 2,068 tons, J. G. Hulphers, master; route same as Old Dominion.

The RICHMOND, iron propellor, freight and passengers, 1,436 tons, Frank Stevens, master; route same as Old Dominion.

The MANHATTAN, iron propellor, freight and passengers, 1,400 tons, —— —— master; route same as Old Dominion.

The BREAKWATER, iron propellor, freight and passengers, 1,110 tons, R. B. Boaz master; route same as Old Dominion.

The HATTERAS, wooden side-wheel, freight, 868 tons, A. B. Mallett, master; route same as Old Dominion.

The ALBEMARLE, wooden side-wheel, freight, 891 tons, —— master; route, same as Old Dominion.

The NORTHAMPTON, wooden side-wheel, freight and passengers, 400 tons, P. McCarrick, master; daily between Norfolk and Old Point, and tri-weekly between Norfolk, Cherrystone, Matthews, Yorktown and Gloucester Point.

The ACCOMACK, wooden side-wheel, freight and passengers, 434 tons, O. G. Delk, master; daily between Old Point and Hampton, and four times a week to Smithfield.

The SHENANDOAH, wooden side-wheel, launched April 11th, 1882, will run on the North Carolina Sounds.

The LURAY, wooden side-wheel, building to run between Norfolk and Newport News.

The NEWBERNE, iron propellor, freight and passengers, 400 tons, T. M. Southgate, master, Norfolk, Newberne and Washington, North Carolina, via Albemarle and Chesapeake Canal.

The PAMLICO, wooden propellor, 252 tons, W. T. Pritchard, master, route same, as the Newberne.

THE MERCHANTS' AND MINERS' TRANSPORTATION COMPANY.

This Company is indeed the peer of any on our seaboard, owning, as it does, the splendid iron steamships running regular between Boston, Providence, Norfolk and Baltimore, besides a number of equally fine vessels engaged in the Northern and Southern trade. Like the Old Dominion Steamship Company, its vessels are the pride of our harbor, and officered by able and experienced seamen, who dock their vessels with characteristic regularity, running to Boston in 48 and to Providence in 36 hours. Their connections to the interior are of course the same as the others, and through bills of lading are issued from either of the cities named to points South, or from the latter to the East and to Europe, over the Cunard, Warren, Leyland and Allen lines.

The spacious wharves at the west end of Main Street, in the centre of that portion of the city now regarded as the most valuable for wharf purposes, and where vast improvements have been made during the last year, are used by the Company, but owned by the corporation known as the BOSTON WHARF AND WAREHOUSE COMPANY.

In advancing the Commercial interests of Norfolk, the merchants' and Miners' Transportation Company have proved an important factor, affording ample and speedy connections between Norfolk and the cities of the North. The vessels owned by the Company are as follows:

The DECATUR H. MILLER, iron propeller, 2,296 tons, Solomon Howes, commander.
The WILLIAM CRANE, iron propeller, 1,416 tons, F. M. Howes, Commander.
The JOHNS HOPKINS, iron propeller, 1,470 tons, Wm. A. Hallett, Commander.
The WILLIAM KENNEDY, wooden propeller, 974 tons, W. E. Warren, Commander.
The BLACKSTONE, wooden propeller, 1,147 tons, John C. Taylor, commander.

The enterprise and good management of the officers of the Company have combined to make it wealthy and powerful, exerting its influence for the best interests of Norfolk. Gen. V. D. Groner is the agent.

THE BALTIMORE STEAM PACKET COMPANY

(OLD BAY LINE.)

This Company owns and operates the most magnificent passenger steamers on the Atlantic coast, and they are the palace steamers of Chesapeake Bay, being new, adapted to a high rate of speed, beautiful in form, substantial in construction, and furnished most sumptiously. With travellers the line is regarded as one of the finest and best in the country, forming the popular trunk route between the North and South. Under the able management of the president, Col. John M. Robinson, assisted by an able corps of competent officers, the Company has become one of the most thoroughly equipped in the country, and proved itself a most powerful adjunct in advancing the best interests of Norfolk. A trip upon either of the passenger boats of the Bay Line is not attended with the fatigue usually incident to ordinary travel.

The Norfolk offices of the Company are on Water Street, in close proximity to the Norfolk and Western Railroad depot, Mr. R. B. Cooke, is the agent; and in Portsmouth the offices of the company are at the depot of the Seaboard and Roanoke Railroad.

The steamers of the Bay Line make close connections at Portsmouth with the regular passenger trains of the Seaboard and Roanoke Railroad, for all points South and South-west, and at Baltimore with the Philadelphia, Wilmington and Baltimore Railroad of Philadelphia, New York and all points North, with the Baltimore and Ohio, Northern Central and Pensylvania Railroad for the North and North-west, with the Allan, Continental, West India and Pacific, Hopper and Johnson steamship Lines for Liverpool; with the Continental for London and North German Lloyds for Bremen. The steamers of the Bay Line are:

The CAROLINA, iron side-wheel, 984 tons, built in 1877; 75 state-rooms, passenger capacity 500, W. C. Whittle, commander.
The FLORIDA, wooden side-wheel, 1,280 tons, built in 1876; 75 state-rooms, passenger capacity 500, A. K. Cralle, commander.
The VIRGINIA, iron side-wheel, 1,300 tons, built in 1879; 80 state-rooms, passenger capacity 500, J. D. Dawes, commander.
The SEABOARD, iron propeller, for freight, 662 tons, L. B. Eddens, commander.
This ROANOKE, iron propeller, for freight, 531 tons, Carter commander.
The TRANSIT, wooden propeller, 475 tons, North, commander.
The WESTOVER, iron propeller,——tons, John S. Eldredge commander.
The GASTON, iron propeller, 846 43-100 tons, for freight, Bloodsworth, commander.

THE CANTON INSIDE LINE.

is a daily fast freight line operated by the Philladelphia, Wilmington and Baltimore Railroad Company in connection with the freight steamers of the Bay Line, between Norfolk, Baltimore, Philadelphia and all points North, having the same connections here as at the Baltimore Steam Packet Company; and at Philadelphia with the American Steamspip Company's steamships for Liverpool and Antwerp. Over these lines through bills of lading are issued.

THE CLYDE LINES.

Of the large steamship interests controlled by Messrs. W. P. Clyde & Co., of 12 South Wharves, Philadelphia and New York, from whom these lines take their name : their New England lines, coast lines to the various States, West Indies and South American ports, it is hardly within our province to treat in this volume. The same enterprising gentlemen have, however, exerted considerable influence in aiding the development of our city and State.

From Norfolk they have a line through the Albemarle and Chesapeake Canal to the different sections of Eastern North Carolina, where they have fostered various auxiliary lines, navigating the smaller streams far into the interior, using boats of lighter draft than heretofore known. These enterprises have largely increased the receipts of cotton at this port from those sections. Their assistance in recognizing and re-establishing the James River Line, when the route was about being given up by the old company, by the aid extended by their Philadelphia line in developing the truck growing sections adjacent to our city, are worthy of mention. They have also taken large interests in different Southern roads, which connect this city and State with the South and Southwest.

At Norfolk the Clyde interests are represented by Captain James W. McCarrick, General Southern Agent, whose office is on the Company's wharves, Water Street. The following vessels comprise Clyde's local fleet :

THE EVERMAN, iron propeller, 696 tons, Jas. A. Smith, master ; Philadelphia and Norfolk.

The NORFOLK, wooden propeller, 500 tons, N. M. Lawson, master ; Baltimore Norfolk and Richmond.

The DEFIANCE, wooden propeller, 400 tons, R. F. Jones master ; Norfolk, Newberne and Washington, N. C.

The STOUT, wooden propeller, 400 tons, W. L. Pierce, master ; Baltimore, Norfolk and Newberne, N. C.

The LOUISA, wooden propeller, —— tons, R. Willis, master ; Baltimore, Washington and Newberne, N. C.

The POINTER, wooden propeller, 1,100 tons. S. C. Platt, master ; Philadelphia, Norfolk and Richmond.

The EXPERIMENT, wooden propeller, 400 tons, R. H. Cannon, master ; Baltimore, Washington and Newberne, N. C.

The FANITA, iron propeller, 454 tons, J. S. Tunnell, master ; Philadelphia, Norfolk and Richmond.

The ASHLAND, wooden propeller, 1,100 tons, Wm. L. Carr, master ; Philadelphia, Norfolk and Richmond.

THE INLAND AND SEABOARD COASTING COMPANY, AND POTOMAC STEAMBOAT COMPANY.

The iron side-wheel steamer "Lady of the Lake," 700 tons, with comfortable accommodations for two hundred and forty passengers, and the "George Leary," run alternately between Norfolk and Washington, D. C., leaving the Boston wharf, west end of Main Street. This is one of the most desirable routes to and from the city, connecting us with our National Capital. During the summer seasons regular excursions over these lines are made by lovers of fresh, invigorating air.

THE VIRGINIA STEAMBOAT COMPANY.
(JAMES RIVER LINE)

The magnificent wooden side-wheel steamer "CITY OF RICHMOND," built in 1880, 1,001 tons, running between Norfolk and Richmond, is the property of this Company It is the finest and swiftest river steamer running in Virginia waters.

The iron side-wheel steamer "ARIEL," 700 tons, also belongs on the James River route, supplying the place of the "City of Richmond" when necessary, making tri-weekly trips between the two cities.

Delightful excursions on these steamers constitute a pleasant feature of their Summer business, passing, as they do, within full view of the oldest historical points connected with the early history of Virginia. Travellers to the Springs of Virginia and West Virginia find the James River Route a convenient and enjoyable one. Captain James W. McCarrick is the local agent of the Company, and L. B. Tatum, Esq., General Superintendent, at Richmond.

NORTH CAROLINA LINES.

The Steamer HARBINGER, Capt. C. H. Johnson, leaves Commerce street wharf every MONDAY at 12 M., and THURSDAY at 6 A. M., for Hertford, Belvidere, N. C., and North river fisheries, and every SUNDAY at 7 A. M., for North river fisheries.

The Steamer CURRITUCK, Capt. J. J. Jones, leaves the wharf, foot of Commerce Street, every WEDNESDAY EVENING for Windsor and all points on the Cashie river, N. C.

The Steamer HELEN SMITH, Capt. J. S. Perry, leaves Commerce Street wharf every TUESDAY, THURSDAY and SATURDAY, 6 A. M., for Blackwater Bridge, Tull's Creek Bridge and all points on A and C. Canal.

The Steamer KEYSTONE, Capt. J. Pugh, will hereafter leave Commerce Street wharf every MONDAY at 6 A. M., for Murfreesboro and all landings on Chowan river.

Under the efficient agency of W. Y. Johnson, Esq., these lines have greatly developed the carrying trade between this city and the fertile sections of North Carolina, bringing to our city the rich products of the Sound region.

THE DISMAL SWAMP CANAL STEAMERS.

These Steamers ply regularly through the Dismal Swamp Canal, and their cargoes are generally very large each way. Capt. Henry Roberts, the energetic and wide awake superintendent of the Canal, is also Superintendent of the Steamboat line, with an office on Taylors wharf, one door west of the Clyde Line wharf. The steamers and their routes, are as follows :

Steamer WM. B. ROGERS, wooden propeller, 70 tons, leaves tri-weely for Elizabeth City and all landings on the Dismal Swamp Canal.

Steamer J. W. HARING, wooden propeller, 40 tons, leaves tri-weekly for Suffolk, Whaleyville and all landings on Nansemond river.

Steamer THOMAS NEWTON, wooden propeller, 70 tons, runs tri-weekly, between Norfolk, Elizabeth City and all landings on Dismal Swamp Canal.

ROANOKE RIVER.

The Steamer LUCY, captain Vincent, with capacity for 300 bales of cotton, leaves Higgins' wharf every Tuesday for all points on Roanoke River. Mr. B. Taylor is agent and also owner.

ROANOKE, NORFOLK AND BALTIMORE STEAMBOAT COMPANY.

(ROANOKE RIVER LINE.)

This company was organized in 1880, the principal executive officers being residents of Williamstown, N. C. Their warehouses and offices are located on the McCullough wharf, W. E. Hudgins agent, and all the steamers, as follows, pass through the Albemarle and Chesapeake Canal.

The CONOHOE, iron propeller, 366 tons, Captain Walker, runs regularly between Baltimore, Norfolk and Roanoke River, stopping at Edenton.

The COMMERCE, wooden propeller, 222 tons, Capt. Latham, runs on the same route.

The ROTARY, wooden propeller, 186 tons, Captain Minter, runs on the same route.

The ASTORIA, iron propeller, 210 tons, Captain Thomas, runs between Norfolk and all points on Roanoke River.

The iron Barges CITY POINT and PETERSBURG are towed, when necessary for freight purposes, by the steamer ROTARY.

These steamers, in addition to their Carolina freight business, take freight between Norfolk and Baltimore, Mr. Robert Tyson, is the agent at No. 4 Spears wharf, Baltimore.

CLYDE'S

Coastwise and West India

STEAM LINES,

BETWEEN

New York and Charleston, S. C.

New York and Wilmington, N. C.

New York, Hayti and San Domingo.

New York and West India Ports.

Philadelphia, Richmond and Norfolk.

Phila., Boston, Providence and Fall River.

Philadelphia and New York.

Philadelphia and Charleston, S. C.

Phila., and Washington, D. C. and Alexandria, Virginia.

Philadelphia, Richmond and Norfolk Line.

WM. P. CLYDE & CO., General Managers,

No. 35 Broadway, New York. - 12 South Wharves, Philadelphia.

JAS. W. McCABRICK, General Southern Agent, Norfolk, Va.

BALTIMORE STEAM PACKET COMPANY.
BAY LINE.

STEAMERS.

FLORIDA,
CAROLINA,
VIRGINIA,
GASTON,

TRANSIT,
ROANOKE,
SEABOARD,
WESTOVER.

Daily Passenger and Fast Freight Route.

BETWEEN BALTIMORE, OLD POINT, NORFOLK, PORTSMOUTH, AND ALL POINTS SOUTH AND SOUTH WEST.

Passenger Steamers leave BALTIMORE daily (except Sundays) from foot of Union Dock, at 7 P.M., and from Canton Wharf at 8:45 P.M., on arrival of Express Train, which leaves NEW YORK at 3:20 P.M., and PHILADELPHIA at 5:30 P.M.

Passengers leave WASHINGTON at 5:30 P.M., connecting with Steamer at Canton Wharf Connect at PORTSMOUTH with Express train, Seaboard and Roanoke Railroad, for all points South.

Going NORTH leave NORFOLK at 4 P.M., PORTSMOUTH, 5:30 P.M., and connects at Canton Wharf, BALTIMORE, with Express train for PHILADELPHIA and NEW YORK, reaching PHILADELPHIA at 11 A.M., and NEW YORK at 1 P.M. BAY LINE also connects at BALTIMORE for WASHINGTON CITY and all points WEST and NORTH-WEST.

THE BAY LINE DAILY FREIGHT ROUTE

Connects BALTIMORE via the Virginia and Tennessee Air Line at NORFOLK, with all points in South Side and South-Western Virginia, Tennessee, Georgia, Alabama and Mississippi; and via the Atlantic Coast Line and Seaboard Air Line at PORTSMOUTH, with all points in North and South Carolina, Georgia and all points South and South-West. Connects NORFOLK AND PORTSMOUTH via Baltimore and Ohio Railroad and Northern Central Railway with all points West, via "NORTH GERMAN LLOYD LINE," with BREMEN, "ALLAN," "CONTINENTAL," "WEST INDIA and PACIFIC," "Hooper and Johnston's" Steamship Lines for Liverpool, "CONTINENTAL" Line for London, Havre; "TULLY Line for London and Newcastle on Tyne—over all of which through Bills of Lading and rates are issued FREIGHT RECEIVED AND FORWARDED TWICE DAILY, EXCEPT SUNDAY.

R. B. COOKE, Agent.

CANTON INSIDE LINE!
ONLY DAILY FREIGHT ROUTE BETWEEN
PHILADELPHIA, NORFOLK AND PORTSMOUTH.

Connecting PHILADELPHIA at NORFOLK via the Virginia and Tennessee Air Line, and at Portsmouth with the Seaboard Air Line and Atlantic Coast Line for all points South and South-West. To insure dispatch, mark and ship your goods via CANTON INSIDE LINE. Goods received in Philadelphia at Depots of P. W. & B. R. R., in Norfolk and Portsmouth at wharves of BAY LINE TRUCK is received for Philadelphia on Tuesdays, Thursdays and Fridays.

☞ For particulars, enquire of

JOHN S. WILSON, GENERAL AGENT.

Dismal Swamp Canal Company,

NORFOLK, VA.

(RE-ORGANIZIED DECEMBER 1st, 1880.)

Connecting the Waters of Chesapeake Bay with Albemarle and Pamlico Sounds, N. C.

The recent extensive improvements by dredging and otherwise, securing a uniform depth of water throughout, recommend this route as a desirable medium of transportation between the waters of Virginia and North Carolina.

OFFICERS:

JNO. B. WHITEHEAD, PRESIDENT.
CAPT. HENRY ROBERTS, SUPERINTENDENT.
S. W. GARY, COLLECTOR.
H. C. WHITEHEAD, SECRETARY AND TREASURER.

DIRECTORS:

W. H. C. ELLIS,   C. W. NEWTON,
          JAMES Y. LEIGH,   CICERO BURRUSS.

DISMAL SWAMP CANAL

STEAMERS,

Office Taylor's Wharf, one door west Clyde's Line,

NORFOLK, VA.

STEAMERS

WM. B. ROGERS AND THOS. NEWTON,

Leave for Elizabeth City and Landings on the Dismal Swamp Canal,

TRI-WEEKLY.

STEAMER J. W. HARRING,

Leaves for Suffolk, Whaleyville and Landings on the Nansemond River,

TRI-WEEKLY.

☞ Freights for all points received daily from 8 A.M. to 6 P.M. Lowest Rates guaranteed.

HENRY ROBERTS, Superintendent.

INLAND NAVIGATION!

THE

ALBEMARLE AND CHESAPEAKE CANAL,

TOGETHER WITH THE

Chesapeake & Delaware Canal & Delaware and Raritan Canal,

FORM THE GREAT INLAND NAVIGATION FROM

NEW YORK, PHILADELPHIA AND BALTIMORE,

TO

NORTH CAROLINA AND THE SOUTH.

BY CANALS AND INLAND NAVIGATION FOR STEAMBOATS, SAILING
VESSELS, RAFTS, &c., AVOIDING THE DANGERS OF HAT-
TERAS AND THE COAST OF NORTH CAROLINA—
SAVING TIME AND INSURANCE.

DIMENSIONS OF CANLS AND LOCKS:

CANALS.	MILES.	LOCKS. Length Feet.	Width Feet	Depth Feet.
Albemarle and Chesapeake Canal - -	14	220	40	7
Chesapeake and Delaware Canal - - -	14	220	24	9
Delaware and Raritan Canal - - -	43	220	24	7
Eric, of New York - - - - - -	345	110	18	7

☞ Light-draft steamers bound to Charleston, Savannah, Florida and the West
Indies take this Route.

Steam tug-boats leave Norfolk, towing sail vessels, barges, rafts, &c., to and from
North Carolina to Baltimore, Philadelphia and New York.

Freight steamers leave Norfolk for the following places: Edenton, Elizabeth City,
Hertford, Plymouth, Jamesville, Williamston, Hamilton, Hill's Ferry, Palmyra, Scot-
land Neck, Halifax, Weldon, Columbia, Fair Field, Windsor, Winton, Gatesville, Murfreesboro, Franklin, Currituck, Coinjock, Roanoke Island, Washington, Greensville.
Tarboro, Indiantown, Bay River and Newberne.

☞ For rates of tolls, towing, maps, charts, &c., apply to

H. V. LESLEY, Treasurer C. & D. Canal Co.,
528 Walnut Street, Philadelphia.

M. COURTRIGHT, Esq.,
Room 45, No. 55 Broadway, New York.

Or to MARSHALL PARKS,
President Albemarle and Chesapeake Canal Co., Norfolk, Va.

THE GREAT
ATLANTIC COAST LINE

Via PORTSMOUTH, VA.

TO AND FROM

Boston, Providence, New York,

PHILADELPHIA, BALTIMORE, NORFOLK,

AND ALL

EASTERN CITIES,

TO ALL POINTS

South and South-West !

Observe the following excellent Schedule of Connections:

BOSTON—Merchants' and Miners' Transportation Company.

PROVIDENCE—Providence, Norfolk and Baltimore Steamship Company.

NEW YORK—Old Dominion Steamship Company.

PHILADELPHIA—Canton Inside Line via P. W. & B. R. R.

BALTIMORE—Baltimore Steam Packet Company.

For further Information apply to

A. POPE, General Passenger Agent.

SOL HAAS, General Freight Agent.

SEABOARD AIR LINE!

Via PORTSMOUTH, VA.

EXPRESS FREIGHT LINE

BETWEEN ALL POINTS

North and South!

STEAMSHIPS TO PORSTMOUTH, THENCE IN THROUGH
CARS VIA RALEIGH, HAMLET, CHARLOTTE,
ATLANTA, AND ALL POINTS SOUTH
AND SOUTH-WEST.

SHIP from the NORTH by the following LINES :

BOSTON—Merchants' and Miners' Transportation Company.
PROVIDENCE—Providence, Norfolk and Baltimore S. S. Co.,
NEW YORK—Old Dominion Steamship Company,
PHILADELPHIA—Philadelphia, Wilmington and Baltimore Railroad,
      "   Clyde Line,
BALTIMORE—Baltimore Steam Packet Company.

For further information apply to

F. W. CLARK, General Agent.

A. POPE,	SOL HAAS,
General Passenger Agent.	General Freight Agent.

THE
ASSOCIATED LINE OF SOUTHERN
RAILWAY TRAVEL,

EMBRACING

The RICHMOND & DANVILLE R.R.
The ATLANTIC COAST LINE
The SEABOARD AIR-LINE

SYSTEM
OF
RAILROADS.

THESE ARE THE

LEADING RAILWAY ROUTES OF THE UNITED STATES

TO THE

SOUTHERN AND SOUTHWESTERN STATES THEREOF,

Composed of operated Railways extending 3,000 miles; traversing the State of Virginia, extending through the States of North and South Carolina into Georgia, Alabama, Mississippi, Louisiana and Texas, and over which special United States Fast Mail and Double Daily Passenger Trains run with extended Pullman Car Service Air-Brakes, and all modern appliances. All-rail connections from New York, Philadelphia, Baltimore, via Washington or via Richmond.

THROUGH TICKETS,
SPECIAL RATES,
CERTAIN CONNECTIONS,
FROM NEW YORK AND ALL EASTERN CITIES,
TO ALL POINTS IN THE
SOUTH AND SOUTH-WEST,
OVER THESE LINES.

The Richmond and Danville System,

Traversing the well-known Piedmont belt of Virginia, and the Carolina, with its stretches of picturesque mountain views and fertile valleys, thence *via* Atlanta to Montgomery, Mobile, New Orleans and Texas, or *via* Charlotte and Columbia to Augusta, Charleston, Savannah, and Florida, saving many miles of travel, and offering superior transportation facilities.

The Virginia Midland Railway,

Controlled and operated by the Richmond and Danville Railroad, which, starting at Washington, penetrates the fairest portions of the Valley of Virginia, and unites at Danville, after a run of 232 miles, with the Richmond and Danville main line, and in many respects offers superior attractions ; Also,

A THIRD ROUTE!

FROM BALTIMORE

VIA CHESAPEAKE BAY TO WEST POINT,

and thence by rail to Richmond, then uniting with the main stem of the Richmond and Danville System; also, another great line :

ATLANTIC COAST LINE

OF RAILWAYS,

Leading via Wilmington to Charleston, Savannah and Florida, with its offer of part water route, should the traveler prefer to avail himself of a night on the Chesapeake Bay from Baltimore to Norfolk.

THE
SEABOARD AIR-LINE

FROM NORFOLK VIA RALEIGH,

Penetrates middle North Carolina, and extends until its union with other portions of the Associated System at Charlotte.

ONE MILLION ACRES

OF

FARMING, GRAZING, VINE-GROWING

AND

MINERAL LANDS

CONTROLLED

BY THE ASSOCIATED RAILWAYS

THROUGH THE LAND BUREAU

OF ITS

PASSENGER DEPARTMENT.

IMMIGRATION.

The cause of Immigration is especially advocated by these lines. Immigrants are invited to occupy the lands we control and reach, and aid in developing the agricultural and mineral resources.

Arrangements have been perfected by which a complete system of settlers' and immigrants' fares from New York and leading Eastern cities exist to each station upon the lines of railway of this organization, and the attention of persons seeking homes, of investors and capitalists is invited to the

MAGNIFICENT
WATER-POWERS,
DEVELOPED AND UNDEVELOPED.
GOLD, SILVER, IRON and OTHER MINES
AND THE
BOUNDLESS FORESTS OF VALUABLE WOODS.

Exhibits (supplied on application), concerning unimproved lands, improved farms, sites for manufacturing purposes, supplies and location of growing hard woods, deposits of minerals, metals and building materials, together with facts of physical attractions, accessibility to RAILWAY OR WATER TRANSPORTATION, and desirable markets.

Full information concerning which, the important points we reach, and in all matters of tickets, time tables, sleeping car reservations, etc., etc., to be had on application to either of the Eastern Agents of the line, viz:

H. P. CLARK, 306 Washington Street, Boston, Mass., 229 Broadway, New York.

B. H. FELTWELL, 1348 Chestnut St., Phila.

A. L. REED, 511 Pennsylvania Avenue, Washington, D. C., or 9 German Street, Baltimore, Md.

N. MACDANIEL, 601 Pennsylvania Ave., Washington, D. C.

Or to the undersigned,

A. POPE,
General Passenger and Ticket Agent,
RICHMOND, VA.

NORFOLK & VIRGINIA BEACH RAILROAD

AND

IMPROVEMENT COMPANY.

This Company, incorporated by the Legislature of Virginia, January, 1882, is making surveys and plans for the construction of a

NARROW-GAUGE RAILWAY

from Norfolk to the sea beach, some **six** miles below Cape Henry and seventeen miles from Norfolk.

THE SEASIDE HOTEL AND LAND CO.,

have purchased nine farms, embracing a territory some five and a half miles in extent, comprising the finest farms in that section and a sea beach that cannot be excelled on the Atlantic coast. The lands are highly productive and furnish all that is required for man or beast. In the rear of these farms are the waters of Lynnhaven, celebrated for oysters and fish.

The property purchased contains several thousand acres and is being laid out into streets, squares and parks, and, as the frontage on the Atlantic is over five miles in extent, ample room will be found for all who may desire to build hotels, cottages, etc. The Railroad will be seventeen miles long, over a level country and nearly straight.

PASSENGER TRAINS WILL REACH THE BEACH IN THIRTY
MINUTES OR LESS FROM NORFOLK.

Parties who may wish to obtain lots for cottages, hotels or club-houses, may address,

MARSHALL PARKS, President.
NORFOLK, VA.

LEADING BANKS, CORPORATIONS,
ℰ BUSINESS HOUSES OF NORFOLK.

In all business centres are to be found individuals and firms who have attained that prominence in business for which their competitors labored unsuccessfully. Some are in the beginning, possessed of large capital and everything favorable to the achievement of success, but through mismanagement, errors in judgment or some of the many hindrances, never become distinguished, except perhaps as failures ; others with energy, enterprise and sterling integrity, win their way until their names become synonyms of success. The firms and corporations- mentioned in the following notices are the most prosperous and progressive in Norfolk.

THE EXCHANGE NATIONAL BANK

Is to-day one of the most prosperous and substantial moneyed institutions in the Southern States. The building, illustrated on page 21, is strikingly handsome, its interior forming one commodious and elegant room, which is furnished with every accessory for expediting and simplifying the business of the bank. The authorized capital is $500,000, of which $300,000 is paid in ; besides it has $150,000 surplus. The bank is also the designated depository and financial agent of the United States. The officers are as follows: Hon. John B. Whitehead, President ; James G. Bain, Vice President ; George M. Bain, Jr., Cashier ; James H. Toomer, Assistant Cashier. (See page 64.)

THE CITIZENS' BANK

Was incorporated in 1867, and like its sister banks, has punctually declared dividends upon its capital stock, bespeaking for the institution an able and judicious management. The directory is composed of wealthy, influential men, who are yet actively engaged in business pursuits, and who appreciate the subject of finance in its most intricate phases. The building of the Citizens' Bank is shown in view of Main Street, page 34 being the second from right-hand corner. The officers are : Wm. H. Peters, President ; Wm. W. Chamberlaine, Vice President ; Walter H. Doyle, Cashier. (See page (66.)

THE MARINE BANK

Was chartered, under our State laws, in June, 1872, and began business at 146 Main Street, subsequently the beautiful granite building, conspicuous in view of Main Street, page 34, was purchased and its interior remodeled for the accomodation of the largely increased business of the bank. The officers and directors are men of acknowledged ability, and under their management the bank has taken high rank. The officers are : Col. Walter H. Taylor, President ; Hugh N. Page, Acting Cashier. (See page 65.)

THE HOME SAVINGS BANK

Is, as the name implies, a savings bank, and was established under charter in 1874. The cash capital of the bank is $20,000, to which is added a surplus of $3,000. The authorized capital is $100,000. Since its organization it has afforded all classes an opportunity to accumulate their smallest earnings, and its success is a matter of congratulation. The building is illustrated on page 32. The officers are : George E. Bowden, President ; George S. Oldfield, Vice President ; H. C. Percy, Cashier, (See page 65.)

THE BANK OF COMMERCE

Was organized under State charter July 1st, 1878, and the building (shown as third from the corner, on page 33) formerly owned by the People's National Bank, on Main at the head of Commerce Street, is devoted to its uses. The Success of the Bank of Commerce has been commensurate with the rapid commercial advancement of the city. The officers are : James E. Barry, President Wm. S. Wilkinson, Cashier. (See page 63.)

E. T. POWELL & SON
WHOLESALE GROCERS.

This firm which succeeded Eastman, Powell & Co., occupies the large and splendid warehouse N. E. corner of Water and Commerce Streets, including Nos. 90 Water and 41 Commerce Streets, fronting on the former 49 and running back 130 feet on the latter. The building is three stories high, affording ample storage capacity. The present firm is composed of two members, Messrs. E. T. & J. R. Powell, the latter having been admitted in July 1881. Being identified with the second largest branch of business in Norfolk, and having an extensive trade in this section, the house stands to-day among the most prominent in Norfolk. (See pages 73 and 74).

M. L. T. DAVIS & CO.,
WHOLESALE GROCERS.

Commenced business in 1865, on Roanoke Square. under firm style of Davis & Bro. After a few years the business of the firm had so increased as to render the provision of greater facilities for its accommodation necessary, when the warehouse S. E. corner of Water and Commerce Streets was built. This building has three floors and basement, 25x100 feet, with an addition in the rear forming an L. About the year 1874 Mr. B. D. Thomas, a former clerk, was admitted to a partnership, and the present firm style adopted. With every facility for the conduct of the business, the firm controls an extensive and excellent trade. (See page 75.)

JAMES M. BUTT,
RAILROAD, STEAMBOAT AND MACHINISTS' SUPPLIES.

This house was established in 1869, the firm name being Forbes, Butt & White, subsequently Forbes. & Butt; the latter was dissolved in 1876 by the death of Mr. N. S Forbes, Mr. James M. Butt succeeding to the business. At the store No. 5 Market square, which is three stories high, 25x70 feet, a large and well assorted stock of all goods pertaining to the business, is kept. The high standing and success of the house is unquestioned. (See page 90.)

E. V. WHITE & CO.,
RAILROAD, STEAMBOAT AND MILL SUPPLIES.

The partners of this firm are Captain E. V. White and Charles Schroeder, both of whom are practical engineers. The partnership was formed in 1873, although the senior member had previously been in the business since 1866, entering in 1869 the Norfolk firm of Forbes, Butt & White, from which he withdrew in 1873 to form the present firm. The senior partner was for several years identified with the trade of Baltimore, traveling as far South as Cuba, and he is the acknowledged originator of this branch in Norfolk. The spirit of enterprise and business energy of the partners have combined to gain for the house a large and satisfactory trade, which continues to increase each year. (See inside of back cover.)

JAMES REID & CO.,
NORFOLK STEAM BAKERY.

This widely known establishment was started in 1856 by Mr. James Reid, and it has since become one of the staunchest manufactories in Norfolk, sending its products to all parts of the country. The Bakery employs the services of between 30 and 40. hands, and has capacity for 100 barrels of flour per day. The salesrooms of the firm are in that beautiful press brick building, shown on page 35, just back of which, on Elizabeth Street, is the factory proper. The materials used in this establishment are always obtained from Norfolk dealers, thus reducing to practice the theory of "Home Patronage." James Reid, W. T. Nimmo and C. C. Reid are the partners. (See page 80.)

FREEMAN, LLOYD, MASON & DRYDEN.
POCOMOKE FERTILIZER MANUFACTURERS.

This firm began business in 1876 at Pocomoke City, Md., under the style of Freeman & Co. In 1880, a branch office was established at Higgins' wharf, in this city. and it is now under the personal direction of the senior partner. During the fall of 1881 the firm erected on the Southern Branch of the Elizabeth river, three and a half miles from Norfolk, the largest fertilizer factory in the South. It contains every appliance known in the manufacture of fertilizers. The building is 90x100 feet square, 4 stories high and contains 27,000 square feet of flooring, Communication with Norfolk is had by steam and sailing vessels, the firm owning both kinds. The factory at Pocomoke is two stories high, fronts 58 feet on Pocomoke river, running back 138 feet and has storage rooms for 1,000 tons of guano. The capacity of the two factories is 150 tons per day. Since this firm has become in part a Norfolk one, its trade in Virginia and the South has grown wonderfully, the superior merits of Pocomoke fertilizer winning for it the highest appreciation among farmers and planters. (See page 96.)

CHARLES REID & SON,
MANUFACTURERS OF STANDARD FERTILIZERS.

This house is one of the old landmarks of our city, having been founded in 1821, Besides being largely engaged in the manufacture of standard brands of fertilizers such as " Farmers' Favorite" and "Farmers' Challenge," both of which are used by our farmers, who recognize in them purity and excellence, the firm does a general commission business, and deals largely in Staves, Treenails, etc. The earliest history of the firm was associated with the stave trade, at one time the largest of the port. The partners are Charles Reid and George C. Reid. The first named is also President of the Board of Harbor Commissioners, and one of the oldest merchants continuously engaged in business in this city. The firm stands to-day, as it has always done, among the most enterprising and successful in Eastern Virginia. The firm's factory is on the Southern Branch, about four miles from the city, near the Gilmerton Lock, on the Dismal Swamp Canal. (See page 97.)

PETERS & REED,
COMMISSION MERCHANTS, STAVE AND LUMBER DEALERS.

This house was established in the year 1855. The present partners are William H. Peters and Washington Reed. Its foreign and coastwise trade is large, and extends to the West India Islands, Liverpool and many Mediterranean ports. Besides the offices on Main Street, Norfolk, the firm controls on the Portsmouth side of the river superior storage and shipping facilities, owning wharf property fronting 226 feet on port warden's line, extending back 380 feet, with two slips, capable of accommodating large ocean steamers. This property is also connected with the S. & R. Railroad by tracks laid across and through its entire length. The exportation of Staves has been carried on successfully and largely by the firm, which is regarded as one of the most reliable and progressive in the City. (See page 114.)

S. A. STEVENS & CO.,
FURNITURE, CARPETING AND PIANOS.

This firm commenced business in 1865 at No. 8 Roanoke avenue, where the business was continued until its volume demanded additional facilities for its accommodation. In response to this demand the firm leased Johnson's Hall, occupying it until 1868, when the elegant and imposing structure corner of Main and Granby Streets was erected by the firm. This building, illustrated on page 39, is three stories high, fronting on Main Street 50 feet, and on Granby Street 130 feet, furnishing 27,000 square feet storage, not including the cellars. The building was recently greatly improved by the addition of the fourth floor and a french roof. The house contains a large and elegant stock, including every variety of Furniture, Floor Coverings, Pianos, etc. The partners are S. A. Stevens and Jerome S. Ames. (See page 68.)

W. F. ALLEN & CO.,
WHOLESALE GROCERS,

Commenced business in 1864. The partners, W. F. Allen and James T. Borum, are also members of the commission firm of Pearce, Allen & Borum, 20 and 22 Commerce Street. The firm's warehouse, corner of Water Street and Rothery's Lane, front 36x200 feet, embracing Nos. 99 Water Street and 18 to 30 Rothery's Lane, where abundant room is had for storing their large and varied stock. The firm is in the full enjoyment of an extensive trade, each season increasing in volume. No changes have occurred in the firm since its original organization. (See page 76.)

T. A. WILLIAMS & DICKSON,
WHOLESALE GROCERS.

The partners of this firm are Theoderick A. Williams and Wm. C. Dickson. The original firm name was T. A. Williams & Co., and Mr. Dickson was for several years a member of the firm, but the present style was not adopted until about January 1st, 1881. The old firm commenced business in 1878. With a keen appreciation of the wants of the trade, Messrs. T. A. Williams & Dickson have established themselves among the most progressive of our business firms. (See page 72.)

THE ELIZABETH IRON WORKS,
CHARLES W. PETTIT, PROPRIETOR.

The business of these works was established by the present proprietor's father in 1854, at the old Gosport Iron Works, and subsequantly removed to 280 and 282 Water Street. The property embraces a very large area, running through one block from Water to Main Streets, fronting 44 feet each way, and it has a depth of 290 feet. The different departments of the Elizabeth Iron Works are supplied with every imaginable kind of machinery necessary to the business. A large force of skilful mechanics is kept steadily employed in the model, boiler, foundry and other rooms. The reputation of the establishment for excellent work, secures for its extensive patronage in Virginia and North Carolina. (See page 112.)

W. A. GRAVES.
STEAM SECTIONAL MARINE RAILWAY, SAW AND PLANING MILLS.

The extensive property known as Graves' Ship-yard, comprising Nos. 209 to 223 Water Street, presents at all times one of the most active scenes to be found in this city. The railway has capacity for vessels of 900 tons register. About 75 caulkers and carpenters are regularly employed. The property fronts on the channel 220 feet and on Water Street 178 feet. Saw and plaining mills are also on the premises, the former are fitted up with every improvement known to the business, including large band saws. The capacity of the mill is from 12,000 to 15,000 feet of board per day. The business was established in 1840. (See page 103.)

JAMES POWER & CO.,
IRON YARD AND METAL HOUSE.

This firm commenced business at its present wholesale stand, 26 and 28 Rowland's wharf, in 1867. The business of the house consists principally of the purchase and sale of new and second hand Machinery, Metals, Chains, Anchors, etc. The purchase of Old Wrecks, Steamers, Vessels, Mills, etc., is made a specialty. On page 40 their principal warehouse is illustrated. (See page 109.)

GEO. W DUVAL & CO.,
NORFOLK IRON WORKS.

This well known firm was organized in 1876, although the senior partner established himself in business in 1858. The partners are George W. Duval and W. H. Ridgewell. Their works are at the northeastern corner of Water and Nebraska Streets, where they manufacture all classes of Machinery, Engines, Boilers, Mills, paying especial attention to every description of steamboat work. The famous Duval Patent Boiler Tube Ferrules are manufactured by them. (See page 108.)

W. F. ALLEN,
WHOLESALE LIQUORS.

With the growth of Norfolk, the business of this house has kept steady pace, until it is the largest and most reliable in the city, in the trade. Mr. Allen is also of the firm of W. F. Allen & Co., Wholesale Grocers, and Pearce, Allen & Borum, Commission Merchants. His stock at No. 99 Water Street, embraces Whiskies, Brandies, Gins, etc., of various makers and vintages, that are known and appreciated by the trade. (See page 69.)

S. N. BRICKHOUSE & CO.,
WHOLESALE BOOTS AND SHOES.

After 21 years active participation in the wholesale trade of this city by the present senior partner, the above firm began business in the massive brick building corner of Water and Commerce Streets (see illustration, page 51), which is three stories high, 30x130 feet, in 1877. From the day of its inception to the present the firm has drawn a large and valuable patronage from the South. The entire stock is always obtained direct from the factories, and selected with special reference to the wants of the Virginia, North Carolina, South Carolina, Georgia and Tennessee Trade, and offered at prices identical with those of Boston or the East. (See page 88.)

REYNOLDS BROS.,
GENERAL MERCHANTS AND SHIPPERS.

This is one of the most enterprising firms engaged in the Foreign trade on the South Atlantic Coast, and it may be said that the Foreign trade of Norfolk has been developed through its enterprise and untiring zeal. The partners are William D. and Henry S. Reynolds, who formed the firm of Reynolds Bros. in 1867, when our export trade was in its infancy. The firm are extensive shippers of Cotton to Liverpool, and a specialty is made of importing salt. The first steamship cleared by the Messrs. Reynolds was the "Brazillian," which left this port for Liverpool in January, 1867, with a cargo of Cotton, Corn, Tobacco, of an aggregate value of $330,000. The wharves and offices of the firm are at Town Point, West end of Water Street, in close proximity to the Cotton centre of the city. The Seaboard Cotton Press, shown on page 25, is the property of this firm, as is also the property known as the "Cotton Exchange Building." In Liverpool, England, the business of the firm is transacted at No. 7 Rumford Street. (See page 87.)

MYERS & CO.,
STEAMSHIP AGENTS AND SHIP BROKERS.

This house was established in 1786 under the name of Moses Myers & Sons, and it did a large business with the West Indies and the Northern of Europe, owning (for those days) large vessels. In 1812 the senior partner became Vice Consul for France, and the firm Frederick Myers & Bros., the senior was then Consul for the Netherlands and Vice Consul for Brazil. At his death in 1832 Mr. Myer Myers succeeded him in these Consulates, and the firm continued in his name until 1840, when his nephew, Moses Myers, was admitted as a partner and the style changed to Myers & Co. In 1856 Mr. Myer Myers became Vice Consul of Great Britain, succeeding the novelist G. P. R. James, and was in turn succeeded by Mr. Barton Myers in 1877 in the Vice Consulates of Great Britain, Netherlands and Brazil. The business of the house has, through the growth of years, become extensive and important. (See Page 87.)

ATLANTIC HOTEL.,
R. S. DODSON, PROPRIETOR.

This magnificent structure stands at the corner of Main and Granby Streets, as shown on page 43. The building fronts on Granby Street 208 feet, has two Ls 140 and 215 feet, one thousand guests find accommodations in the present building. Two passenger elevators connect the different floors, besides wide and easy rising stairways lead from pit to roof in several parts of the house. Mr. Dodson has made the Atlantic the *palace* hotel of the South ; certainly none in the cities of this State equal it. The house is furnished with gas made upon the premises from a machine having capacity of 3,000 feet per day. Mr. Dodson was at the well known Maltby House, Baltimore, from 1856 to 1859, the Fountain from 1859, to 1869, and at the Herdic House, Williamsport, and Minnequa Spring, Pa., from 1869 to 1871, when he moved to Norfolk. He also leased the Ocean View Hotel season before last. (See page 58.)

PURCELL HOUSE,
R. T. JAMES, PROPRIETOR.

This was originally the old and popular National Hotel, distinguished for its excellence then, as it is now, although the building has been so thoroughly improved and altered that it does not resemble its former self except in size. The changes have modernized and beautified it. It is to-day one of the best furnished and most comfortable hotels anywhere, affording every convenience, while the *cuisine* is of the very best character. Mr. R. T. James, present proprietor, assumed the proprietorship in the Fall of 1878, and under his direction the house was refurnished and fitted up. Electric call bells , elevators and nicely carpeted wide stairways connect the five floors. The house has accommodations for 250 guests, Illustrated on page 37. (See page 60.)

JORDAN HOUSE,
AMOS P. JORDAN, PROPRIETOR.

No. 30 Market Square, was opened January 1st, 1878, and is conducted on the American and European plans. Mr. Jordan, the proprietor, is an experienced caterer and he has made his house popular with a large number of people who visit the city. The prices of the house are low, while the table is supplied with everything in season. (See page 62.)

HYGEIA HOTEL, OLD POINT,
H. PHOEBUS.

When we speak of a Summer resort we do not intend always to convey the idea that it is a pleasure or health resort, but when we mention the Hygeia Hotel, at Old Point, we mean both. It is also a splendid Winter sanitarium, and the house is never without a very large number of guests, from January to December. It has 21,000 square feet of verandas encircling the house, 6,000 feet are encased in glass for the special use of guests who prefer seeing the breeze to feeling it. An illustration on page 9 shows a distant view of the hotel. (See page 59.)

WALKE & WILLIAMS.
DRUGS, PAINTS AND OILS.

This firm, composed of Dr. F. A. Walke and J. N. Williams, succeeded to the old established business of A. E Wilson & Co., Roanoke Avenue and Water Street, in 1874. The house does a large wholesale trade in Virginia and North Carolina, supplying country, merchants and physicians with everything they need in Drugs, Paints, Oils, etc. (See page 81.)

M. A. & C. A. SANTOS,
DRUGS, PAINTS, OIL, ETC.

Founded in 1819, this house is now in its 63rd year; venerable in years, youthful in its vigor, maintaining its position among the leading and successful enterprises of to-day. The large and handsome store shown on page 41, corner of Main and Atlantic Streets, is filled with the richest and most elegant articles usually kept in our best Drug Stores. Apart from articles of a Medical nature. Toilet and Fancy Articles in large variety are kept in stock and sold to the wholesale and retail trade at Northern or Eastern prices. The store fronts on Main 25 and on Atlantic Street 120 feet. (See page 82.)

PERRY & JERNIGAN,
COTTON FACTOR AND COMMISSION MERCHANT,

Entered the commission business in May 1881, and succeeded to the firms of G. W. McGlauhon & Co., McGlauhon & Norman, McGlauhon & Perry, and J. W. Perry. On May 1st, 1882, T. R. Jernigan, of Hertford, N. C., became a member of the firm. Their warehouse, on Tunis' Wharf, is in close proximity to rail and water transportation and 1,600 bales of Cotton can be easly stored in it. The sale of Cotton is a special feature of the business, which is wholly Commission. (See page 121.)

PEARCE, ALLEN & BORUM,
COTTON FACTORS AND COMMISSION MERCHANTS.

Messrs. S. F. Pearce, Wm. F. Allen and Jas. T. Borum, the two last named who are also partners under firm style of W. F. Allen & Co., Wholesale Grocers, constitute this firm, which was formed in 1878. The senior partner has been in the Commission business here 11 years. Their warehouse, including Nos. 20 and 22 Commerce Street, is 40x70 feet, three stories high, and supplies convenient and abundant storage. The house pays special attention to the sale of Cotton, Grain, Lumber, Peanuts and Produce generally. (See page 122.)

C. HALL WINDSOR.
BOOKS, STATIONERY, ETC.

The assortment of goods displayed at this store exceeds in quality and completeness that of any other in the city. The place, No. 5 Bank Street, is the popular resort of all who desire to obtain fine Stationery, Blank Books, etc., for merchants, students or ladies.. (See page 93.)

NORFOLK CITY MILLS,
LYMAN & Co., PROPRIETORS.

This mill is located on Smith's Creek, just within the corporation limits of the city. It is fitted up with one 100 house power engine, 7 runs of burrs and 3 sets of rolls for manufacturing new process flour. Its capacity is equal to 100 barrels of flour, 500 bushels of meal per day. This property was at one time owned by the late firm of George K. Goodridge & Co. The commodious warehouse of the firm is upon Hardy's wharf, where cargoes can be cheaply and quickly handled. Lyman & Co.'s principal brands of flour are the "Old Dominion," and " Purity," both of which equal the Minnesota brands established 20 years ago. For enterprise and liberality this firm is conspicuous. The Partners are N. E. Lyman, J. M. Lyman, C. G. Lyman and B. S. Cook. (See page 78.)

J. Z. LOWE,

WHOLESALE AND RETAIL GROCER,

Occupies building southeast corner Union Street and Market Square, including Nos. 1, 3 and 5 Union Street and 13 and 15 Market Square, where he carries a fine assortment of Family Groceries, Ship Stores, Wines, Liquors, etc., adapted to a first class trade. (See page 77.)

GEORGE TAIT,

SEEDSMAN.

In the year 1869 Colonel George Tait founded the seed business which he now so successfully conducts at No. 7 Market Square. All seeds offered by this house are grown especially for it in Germany, England, France, Canada and parts of the United States, all orders being given just one year in advance of delivery. Purity and vitality are the two chief merits claimed for Tait's seeds, and with 33 years practical experience the means by which these two important elements may be secured , are thoroughly understood. (See page 79.)

JOSEPH KLEPPER,

RHINE WINE ROOMS AND SUMMER GARDEN,

This establishment, 143 and 145 Church Street, so well known to frequenters of local places of resort and amusement, has recently undergone many improvements. The main and billiard halls (the latter the best in the city), beautifully frescoed, and the entire premises, covering an area of 6,000 square feet, put in complete order for the Summer season. The different departments are connected by lattice walled walks, and the billiard room is so constructed that it can be closed tightly in Winter, or its sides changed into lattice work in Summer. Orchestrion concerts, upon one of the finest instrument of its kind in the South, are given each evening, and instrumental entertainments at intervals through the week. (See page 70.)

H. R. WOODIS.

WINES, LIQUORS, CIGARS, ETC.

At No. 8 Bank Street Mr. Woodis offers a select and elegant stock of goods, comprising the finest Imported and Domestic Wines, Liquors, Cigars, Condiments, etc. The place is favorably known as the "Tip-Top" Wine and Liquor Store. (See page 71.)

JOHN VERMILLION,

WINES, CIGARS, ETC.

The large and varied assortment of Imported Wines, Cigars, Porter, Ale, etc., kept in stock at the above store, No. 4 Granby Street, under the Atlantic Hotel, is of the best quality and manufacture. The purest goods only are kept. With a full line of select customers Mr. Vermillion enjoys an excellent trade. (See page 71.)

LUTHER SHELDON,

SASH, DOORS AND BLINDS.

The business of this house, which was established in 1870, has grown to be very extensive and far-reaching. The building illustrated on inside cover, now occupied by Mr. Sheldon, runs from No. 49 Roanoke Avenue, through the centre of the block to 16 West Side Market Square; contains four floors, including basement, 25x200 feet, with elevators, speaking tubes and phones connecting the different stories. The establishment is the largest of its kind in this section, and it represents the controlling agencies of large manufacturing mills. (See inside front cover.)

A. M. VAUGHAN & SON,

INSURANCE AGENTS,

Represent at their Agency, 96 Main Street, reliable Foreign, Domestic, Fire, Life and Marine Insurance Companies. With an established line of Insurance and perfectly solvent Companies, they do an extensive business. (See page 99.)

C. T. JORDAN & BRO.,
CLOTHING AND GENTS' FURNISHINGS.

This firm, composed of C. T. and A. E. Jordan, succeeded the original firm of C. T. & L. W. Jordan, at 124 Main Street. Besides carrying a fine stock of ready-made Men's and Children's Clothing and Gent's Furnishing Goods, the house represents the tailoring establishments of Jessup & Co. and Devlin & Co., New York. (See page 103.)

NOTTINGHAM & WRENN,
ICE, COAL AND WOOD DEALERS.

The wharf known as Nottingham & Wrenn's, Atlantic City, fronts on property covering 5½ acres, with 330 feet deep water front and 614 feet depth, extending back to the bridge connecting the village of Atlantic City with Norfolk. The premises of the firm, which is composed of Thomas T. Nottingham and William A. Wrenn, and which was organized in 1876, contains the very best facilities for the accommodation of their immense trade in Ice, Coal and Wood. The ice house affords storage for 4,000 tons, and the coal yard is supplied with all grades of Coal. Five large oyster packing houses stand upon this property, among them that of the Union Oyster Company, the largest oyster packing concern in the United States. Recently Messrs. Nottingham & Wrenn purchased a valuable piece of wharf property in Edenton, N. C., where they will conduct the ice and coal business in all its branches. This depot was rendered necessary by their largely increased business with Eastern Carolina. Extensive buildings are being erected by the firm. At Nos. 6 and 7 Campbell's wharf the firm has a branch office. (See page 116.)

MANEELY'S ART STUDIO.

This studio is the recognized headquarters for fine photographic, crayon, water-color or india-ink work. All the work turned out of the establishment is finished in a manner unequalled, except by the best artists in the country. (See page 103.)

W. A. ANDERSON,
OLD ATLANTIC FOUNDRY.

Twelve years ago Mr. Anderson inaugurated the business which he now so successfully conducts at 206 Water Street. In 1876 he erected a substantial brick building, 60x50 feet, fronting on a yard 75x100 feet. Adjoining the Foundry is a 30 horse-power engine; and the establishment engages 12 hands. The heaviest casting made here in 1880, weighed 4,300 pounds. Mr. Anderson is now building an extensive Machine Shop, to be supplied with all kinds of modern machinery necessary in making Steam Engines, Boilers, Saw and Grist Mills, &c. (See page 107.)

BUTT & CO.,
WHITE BRONZE MONUMENTS.

For memorial purposes the material known as White Bronze is the most imperishable. It approaches nearer the dark bronze of antiquity than any other material. It is beautiful in color, will not corrode or become moss covered, and it has been known to stand over *three hundred years*. A great mistake is made by persons who think the White Bronze contains iron. It is of pure zinc and other metals known only to the manufacturers. The designs in White Bronze can be rendered more beautiful and in accord with the purchasers wishes than any other, while the price is comparatively low. The writer of this notice knows whereof he speaks, when he declares White Bronze the handsomest, cheapest and most substantial substance for monuments, statuary medallions, etc., ever used. Scientists pronounce it so, and experience has proved it so. Messrs. Butt & Co, are also agents for the Patent Combination Wrought Iron Railings, the handsomest and most durable style of railing now in the market. (See page 110.)

NORFOLK COLLEGE FOR YOUNG LADIES.

This institution of learning was founded by a stock company of which Mr. John L. Roper is President, Kader Biggs, vice President, R. H. Wynne, Secretary, and W. S. Wilkinson, Treasurer. It is the first college in this section organized in the manner stated, and its success has been without a parellel in the history of Virginia colleges. An able corps of teachers preside over each department. The building (see illustration) corner of Granby and Washington Streets, is both beautiful and substantial, while its interior, with every appliance needed in the school work, renders it as complete as any in the country. The course of study embraces three departments, the Primary, Intermediate and Collegiate. Ample provision is made for thorough instruction in all the studies from the most elementary to the highest. (See page 92.)

W. H. SMITH & SON,
COMMISSION MERCHANTS.

This house is among the oldest in the city, standing among the most progressive and enterprising. The purchase and exportation of staves constitute a large share of the firms business. (See page 121.)

W. W. GWATHMEY & CO.,
COMMISSION MERCHANTS.

The extensive warehouse at Town Point, known as "Gwathmey's Warehouse," is the property of this firm. The firm does a general commission and bonded warehouse business. The partners are W. W. Gwathmey, Chas. G. Elliott and Temple Gwathmey. (See page 122.)

JOHN O. GAMAGE,
BUILDERS' MATERIAL.

The above business was founded in 1865, when our people were just beginning to recover from the terrible effects of war, and it has become an established success. Mr. Gamage's facilities for supplying all classes of Building Material are unsurpassed. At his warehouse, 100 and 102 Water Street, he carries a large and varied stock. (See page 83.)

RAWLINS, WHITEHURST & CO,
ICE DEALERS.

Partners, Wm. Rawlins, C. H. Whitehurst, J. M. Haynes, H. A. De Witt and Ira D. Sturgis. In 1869 the firm of Rawlins, Baum & Co. was organized, the present firm succeeding to the business in 1874. The three last mentioned partners look after the firm's business in Maine. They handle between 8,000 and 10,000 tons of Ice per season and ship as far South as Cuba. Their city trade requires the use of 6 wagons, and they make a specialty of furnishing the fisheries in this State and North Carolina. Situated on Biggs' wharf, Nivison Street, conveniently to the different water and land transportation lines their shipping facilities are unsurpassed. (See page 117.)

J. G. TAYLOR & CO.,
BILLIARD TABLE MANUFACTURERS, BALTIMORE.

The success of this house and its rapid growth in popular favor has not been equalled by that of any other in the same business in the Southern States. Messrs. Taylor & Co.'s Billiard Tables are known and appreciated for their durability, elegance of finish, elasticity of cushions and general workmanship. Recently Messrs. Taylor & Co. moved their manufactory and salesrooms to 367 West Baltimore Street, nearly opposite the Eutaw House, where space and location are excellently adapted to the requirements of their business. (See page 100.)

THAYER'S STABLES.
JAMES W. THAYER, PROPRIETOR,

These are the popular hiring stables of Norfolk, where can be had Horses, Buggies, Carriages and every description of vehicle, from the ordinary wagon to the handsomest and newest style Carriage. A specialty is made of furnishing weddings, private parties and funerals. (See page 99.)

B. TAYLOR,
COMMISSION MERCHANT.

This house was established in 1875, and has ever since been actively engaged in the general shipping and commission business. The warehouse, on Higgin's wharf has storage capacity for 1,000 bales of cotton, while the wharf room can conveniently hold 20,000 shingles. The steamer "Lucy," which runs to all points on Roanoke River, is owned and operated by Mr. Taylor. (See page 135.)

G. & R. BARRETT.
WHOLESALE GROCERS.

This firm began business in 1871, beginning on Dinwiddie Street, Portsmouth, and on January 1st, 1882, the business was removed to the extensive warehouse corner of Water Street and Roanoke Square, Norfolk. This warehouse is four stories high, has extensive fronts on both avenues, and contains a well assorted stock of groceries adapted to the jobbing trade. The partners are George H. and Robert H. Barrett. (See page 76.)

THE BERGNER & ENGEL BREWING CO. OF PHILADELPHIA.

This company, with one exception, the largest in the world, in 1881, established a supply depot on Madison Street, near Clyde Line wharves, where was erected a well appointed Ice House, with capacity for storing between 400 and 500 barrels of beer, requiring the constant use of 200 tons of ice. All of the Clyde steamers contain ice boxes built expressly for transporting the Bergner & Engel Company's beer. This city is the supply point for Eastern Virginia, and a large part of the South-east. Mr. F. W. Adams, the energetic and well known manager of this department, whose office adjoins the Refrigerator depot, looks after the company's business in this section. The sales of the company in 1882, will probably reach 200,000 barrels. (See page 70.)

W. B. ROGERS & CO,
FURNITURE DEALERS.

This well known and reliable house began business at Johnson's Hall, 184 and 186 Main Street, September 1st, 1880. The building is one of the largest and most imposing in the city, being 60x189 feet square. The principal salesroom the largest in the South, is 60x90 feet, 38 feet pitch, with a wide balcony encircling it. The ceilings and walls are handsomely frescoed. An upper wareroom is 60x30 feet. The entire shipping and receiving is done from the rear entrance of the establishment. The stock of the house is of the finest quality, while the prices are guaranteed as low as those of any other first-class establishment. The partners are Col. Wm. B. Rogers and V. Paul Jordan. (See page 67.)

P. WILLS,
FINE BOOTS AND SHOES.

Began the present business, No. 84 Main Street, Academy of Music Building, December 3rd, 1881. A branch store for the sale of cheaper goods has been opened at No. 266 Church Street. The stock comprises every variety and grade, especial attention being paid to ladies and misses fine goods. (See page 89.)

WEBB, JETT & COX,
DRUGS, PAINTS, OILS, &c.

This firm was organized under the style of Webb & Jett, August 1st, 1881, and on February 15th, 1882, Mr. W. W. Cox was admitted to an interest and the firm name changed to its present style. Their stock is large and varied, consisting of Drugs, Paints, Oils, Glass, Toilet Articles, &c., a specialty, being made of New Jersey enameled paint, conceded to be without an equal. They are also agents for Powell's Prepared Chemicals, for fertilizing purposes. The partners are R. W. Webb, Jetson Jett and W. W. Cox. (See page 82.)

C. H. N. MASON,
PAPER WAREHOUSE.

This house, the only one dealing exclusively in paper, was established at No. 19 Main Street, about June 15th, 1881. The warerooms contain a full line of wrapping and printers papers, fancy papers, bags, stationery, &c. The agencies for Pennsylvania Pulp and Paper Company, which turns out from 15 to 20 tons of paper per day, and the Acme Blank Book Factory, the reputation of which extends all over the country. Mr. Mason is the first to successfully engage in this particular line of business in the city, and he caters expressively for the wholesale trade, making a specialty of roll paper, which is especially adapted to building purposes, being a substitute for plaster. He does an extensive business, and besides the agencies enumerated, he represents the famous Manilla Paper Manufacturers, D. P. Walton & Co., of New York. (See page 102.)

OCEAN VIEW,
THE CONEY ISLAND OF VIRGINIA.

This delightful Summer resort, where old ocean beats with force upon a firm sand beach, and where the finest, most palatable fish in the world are caught within a stones throw of the doors; with its extensive and delightful surroundings, is again open for the accommodation of those who seek health or pleasure during the Summer months. The management is under Mr. J. A. Kennedy, whose proprietorship last season established for Ocean View a reputation which drew patrons from all parts of the country. With every facility and luxury of a first-class city hotel, it enjoys the additional advantage of being directly upon the beach, where the cooling ocean breezes render the warmest days refreshing and invigorating. A ride of twenty minutes carries one to or from the city, the distance being eight miles, with regular trains every two hours. The rooms at Ocean View are airy and elegantly furnished, while the appointments of the whole house are of the best character; while the rates are as reasonable as those of any first-class watering place in this State. In local parlance, Ocean View is termed the "Coney Island" of Virginia. (See page 61.)

HANNAN & KELLY,
SALE AND COMMISSION STABLES.

These stables, located at Nos. 40, 42 and 44, Union, and No. 64 Church Streets, are the largest in Eastern Virginia, and the proprietors, Messrs. William Hannan and John Kelly, are the recognized leaders in their branch of business. They make a specialty of Northern and Western stock, which they sell at private sale. The stables are two story and easily accommodate 300 head of horses. (See page 99.)

NORFOLK AND VIRGINIA BEACH RAILROAD AND IMPROVEMENT CO.
COMMODORE MARSHALL PARKS, PRESIDENT.

This Company, incorporated by the Legislature of Virginia, January, 1882, is making surveys and plans for the construction of a narrow-gauge railway from Norfolk to the sea beach, some six miles below Cape Henry and seventeen miles from Norfolk. The Seaside Hotel and Land Company have purchased nine farms, embracing a territory some five and a half miles in extent, comprising the finest farms in that section, and a sea beach that cannot be excelled on the Atlantic coast. The lands are highly productive and furnish all that is required for man or beast. In the rear of these farms are the waters of Lynnhaven, celebrated for oysters and fish.

The property purchased contains several thousand acres and is being laid out into streets, squares and parks, and as the frontage on the Atlantic is over five miles in extent, ample room will be found for all who may desire to build hotels, cottages, etc. The railroad will be seventeen miles long, over a level country and nearly straight. Passenger trains will reach the beach in thirty minutes or less from Norfolk. Parties who may wish to obtain lots for cottages, hotels or club-houses, may address the president. (See page 146.)

———————— ♦ ————————

NOTE—For corporations and firms not mentioned here see general index.

———————— ♦ ————————

EATON & BURNETT,
BUSINESS COLLEGE, BALTIMORE.

This institution stands at the head of the list of business colleges in the United States, where the most thorough training in mathematics, penmanship and all departments of bookkeeping, qualifies the student for an active career in the marts of trade and finance. Prof. Burnett, the senior principal, has spent many years in training the young men of the South, and throughout the country may be found business men of prominence, who have graduated under his care. As a penman, Prof. E. Burnett, is without a rival.

Mr. Eaton, a gentleman of acknowledged ability as an instructor, is Prof. Burnett's partner—principal, and with him superintends the operations of the college, corner of Baltimore and Charles Streets. (See back cover.)

UNIVERSITY OF VIRGINIA.

The session of this institution begins on the first of October, and continues until the Thursday before the fourth day of July ensuing. (See page 91.)

SOUTHERN SHIRT MANUFACTORY,
R. H. ANDERSON & CO., RICHMOND, VA.

This business was established in 1876. Only skilful cutters and operatives, who are thoroughly experienced in their respective departments are employed, while the entire work, from preparing the crude goods to finishing, is done under the supervision of the proprietors. The principal room used by the firm is the finest in the city, devoted to commercial purposes, being 60x65 square and 25 feet pitch. Wamsutta, G. B. Langhorn, Utica Nonpareil Cottons, and the best grades of linens direct importation are used in manufacturing. (See page 102.)

THE UNITED STATES MERCANTILE REPORTING AND COLLECTION ASSOCIATION.

The Association, founded by the leading Manufacturers, Importers and Jobbers of New York, has gradually grown until its correspondents or offices are in every post office or city in the United States. Its system of collections and reports are original with the Secretary and Manager, Mr. William Gregory Jones, whose headquarters are at No. 335 Broadway, New York. (See page 115.)

BOSTON BELTING CO.,
MANUFACTURERS OF RUBBER GOODS, BOSTON, MASS.

The Boston Belting Co., is the oldest and by far the largest company in the United States, devoted to the manufacture of Rubber Goods. It was incorporated in 1845, and at various mechanical exhibitions held in this country the merits of its goods have invariably secured for them the highest awards by medal or diploma. The specialties of the company are too numerous to mention here, but they include every article made of rubber for mechanical uses. The officers of the company are : E. S. Converse, President ; Wm. H. Furber, Treasurer and General Manager ; J. B. Forsyth, Manufacturing Agent, with principal offices 222 to 226 Devonshire Street, Boston, and 70 Reade and 112 Duane Streets, New York. (See page 101.)

H. M. SMITH & CO., RICHMOND, VA,

This old house continues in the front rank in the agricultural implement line. It was established in 1829, and has maintained its position as the leading one in the South in the implement trade. They have just issued their catalogue for 1882, a mammoth pamphlet of 200 pages. This increase in the size of their catalogue is necessitated by the constantly increasing stock and variety of goods. They have recently added Steam Engines, and Saw Mills, Grist Mills, and Cotton Gins, to their former variety, and have increased their line of Farm and Freight Wagons. In this line they represent the celebrated Studebaker Bros., Mitchel, Lewis & Co., and Listo Bros., three of the largest Wagon Manufacturing firms in the world. All goods bought of this house may be depended upon to be exactly as represented. The firm consists of H. M. Smith, the founder of the business, I. S. Tower and J. T. Smith. The two younger partners have been with the house since 1858. Of all the firms in the South in their line, Messrs. H. M. Smith & Co., are regarded the most progressive and enterprising. Their goods are known and appreciated for their merit, and they are used in almost every agricultural community South of Maryland. (See page 111.)

GENERAL INDEX.

INDEX TO ILLUSTRATIONS.

INDEX TO ADVERTISEMENTS.

9 7 8 3 7 4 4 7 3 5 7 8 0